W9-CBC-613

This book is from

the kitchen library of

_____

_____

ALSO BY ART GINSBURG, **Mr. Food**®

The **Mr. Food**® Cookbook, *OOH IT'S SO GOOD!!*® (1990)

Mr. Food® Cooks Like Mama (1992)

Mr. Food® Cooks Chicken (1993)

Mr. Food® Cooks Pasta (1993)

Mr. Food® Makes Dessert (1993)

Mr. Food® Cooks Real American (1994)

Mr. Food®**'s** Favorite Cookies (1994)

Mr. Food®**'s** Quick and Easy Side Dishes (1995)

Mr. Food® Grills It All in a Snap (1995)

Mr. Food®**'s** Fun Kitchen Tips and Shortcuts (and Recipes, Too!) (1995)

Mr. Food®**'s** Old World Cooking Made Easy (1995)

"Help, **Mr. Food**®! Company's Coming!" (1995)

Mr. Food® Pizza 1-2-3 (1996)

Mr. Food® Meat Around the Table (1996)

Mr. Food® Simply Chocolate (1996)

Mr. Food® A Little Lighter (1996)

Mr. Food® From My Kitchen to Yours: Stories and Recipes from Home (1996)

Mr. Food® Easy Tex-Mex (1997)

Mr. Food® One Pot, One Meal (1997)

Mr. Food® Cool Cravings (1997)

Mr. Food®**'s** Italian Kitchen (1997)

Mr. Food® Simple Southern Favorites (1997)

Mr. Food® A Taste of QVC: Food & Fun Behind the Scenes (1998)

A
Mr. Food®
CHRISTMAS

Homemade and Hassle-Free

Mr. Food®
Art Ginsburg

WILLIAM MORROW AND COMPANY, INC.
NEW YORK

Library of Congress Cataloging-in-Publication Data

Ginsburg, Art.
A Mr. Food Christmas: homemade and hassle-free / Mr. Food, Art
Ginsburg. —1st ed.
p.   cm.
Includes index.
ISBN 0-688-15679-7
1. Christmas cookery.   I. Title.
TX739.2.C45G53   1998
641.5'68—dc21   98-37986
                     CIP

Printed in the United States of America

First Edition

1 2 3 4 5 6 7 8 9 10

BOOK DESIGN BY MICHAEL MENDELSOHN AT MM DESIGN 2000, INC.

www.williammorrow.com

www.mrfood.com

Foreword

I must admit, when I heard that Mr. Food was finally writing a Christmas cookbook, I let out a giant sigh of relief. You see, Mrs. Claus and I are big Mr. Food fans, and we've prepared his quick-and-easy recipes many times, especially around the holidays, when we pull those all-nighters and need to feed all our hungry helpers in a hurry!

My job isn't easy (but I'm not complaining!), and when it comes to getting a meal on the table, Mrs. Claus and I need to work fast so we can get back to our other important duties. Just think about all there is to do—all year long there are children to watch over, toys to make, and a flight plan to map out for The Big Night. Even Santa Claus needs a little help now and then. Thank goodness for Mrs. Claus, the elves, and now, Mr. Food.

When I heard about *A Mr. Food Christmas, Homemade and Hassle-Free,* all I could say was a hearty "Ho, Ho, Ho!" It's safe to say that when it comes to food, I'm an expert in one particular area: eating! And because I know how helpful Mr. Food's always been with his quick recipes and tips, I couldn't wait to dig into some of the goodies he came up with for this book in celebration of my favorite time of the year.

Yes, this new Mr. Food cookbook really is filled with everything you'll need to make your holiday homemade and hassle-free. Of course there's one chapter that's my personal favorite . . . Cookie Exchange. Surprised? Maybe now would be a good time to ask you a favor: Would you please take special note of those recipes?

Well, I'd better be getting back to my workshop and the things I do best, like finding out who's been naughty and who's been nice.

But before I go, I'll let you in on a secret: Mr. Food is definitely on my nice list this year because, thanks to his new cookbook, he's become one of Santa's best helpers. (And he can be one of yours, too!) Oh, yes—I sure do love that greeting of his! And, speaking of greetings, Ho, Ho, Ho . . . Merry Christmas, everybody!

Acknowledgments

I had so much fun putting together this book! It was as if I had traded in my chef's hat for a bright red Santa hat. For months after the holidays had ended, my kitchen was transformed into the North Pole—with surprise goodies streaming out of it every day. Instead of listening to the radio while we worked, we played Christmas carols throughout the office to make the holiday mood last long after everybody's trees and decorations had been taken down.

You know, all this joy and cheer couldn't have been possible without the entire Mr. Food team. They helped create this book and make it a truly hassle-free experience for me.

Just like the team of reindeer who lead the way, Howard Rosenthal and my daughter Caryl Ginsburg Fantel were always on hand with their ideas (not their noses!) shining brightly. And I appreciate all the organizational support they had from the talented and efficient Larissa Lalka and Charlie Tallant.

I thank the capable elves in my test kitchen: Patty Rosenthal, the veteran of the group; Cheryl Gerber, whose smile has more sparkle than any Christmas tree; Cela Goodhue, who's as dependable as Santa on Christmas Eve; and Janice Bruce, who is a constant source of new ideas. Under the guidance of Joe Peppi, they meticulously tested and tasted each recipe with me to make sure it would meet Santa's (and my) strict guidelines.

Just as Christmas wouldn't be Christmas without decorations, my office wouldn't be nearly as productive without a number of other talented folks, and I thank them, too: my son Steve, who, just as Santa watches over his toy shop, watches over our entire company to make sure things run smoothly; my son Chuck, who handles our TV station relations with his able assistant, Alice Palombo; Chet Rosenbaum, who keeps better track of our finances than an air traffic controller does of Santa's sleigh on Christmas Eve; Tom Palombo, our determined licensing director, and his enthusiastic assistant, Heidi Triveri; Marilyn Ruderman, who keeps my schedule straight (and that's no easy job!); Helayne Rosenblum, my creative script assistant; Carol Ginsburg, my clever editorial assistant; Robin Steiner, our very merry administrative assistant; and Beth Ives, our customer relations supervisor, who knows just how to help everybody who writes to me! As always, I thank my wife, Ethel, for being an invaluable part of the whole picture.

That's just the beginning of my thank-you list! There's my agent, Bill Adler, who helps turn my ideas into gifts for everyone to enjoy year-round. And there are lots of people at William Morrow I can't thank enough for their support: Bill Wright, President and CEO of the Hearst Book Group; Michael Murphy, Morrow Publisher and Senior Vice President; and Senior Editor Zachary Schisgal. Richard Aquan, Nikki Basilone, Claire Israel, and Jackie Deval are all first-string players on the team, too. And I certainly can't leave out ever-willing-to-go-the-extra-mile designer Michael Mendelsohn of MM Design 2000, Inc.

This is the first book I've done with color photos throughout—and each dish is more inviting-looking than the last! Many thanks to Dave Tinsch of Fashion Plates as well as Jean Suits and Patty Rosenthal for handling all the details and working with me on the food for the photos taken at the Hal Silverman Studio. My warmest appreciation to Hal and the gang at his studio: Rick Needle, Frank Schram, and Nancy Nosiglia.

Last but certainly not least, thanks to Karen Fonner, Paula Piercy, Jo Ann Kurz, and all my other friends at QVC who make sure we make the most of every QVC visit.

As I wrap up my thank-yous to all the people mentioned above, plus the wonderful companies and individuals listed below, I thought I'd leave you with my wishes for you, expressed in this fun twist on a Christmas favorite: " 'Twas the night before Christmas and all through the house, not a creature was stirring—'cause everybody was in bed dreaming of all the upcoming '*OOH IT'S SO GOOD!!*®' "

Bob Baniak and Sharon & Rick Delles,
    for providing Christmas props
Bobs® Candies, Inc., for providing a rainbow of candy canes
Christmas Place, Fort Lauderdale, Florida
Hershey Foods Corporation, for providing holiday chocolates
Katie, for sharing some of her favorite recipes
Party Express, a division of Hallmark Cards,
    for providing invitations, partyware, and napkins
Julie Suits, for sharing her baking expertise
Taylor Rental, for providing party supplies
Yankel & Company Catering/Traditions Restaurant

Contents

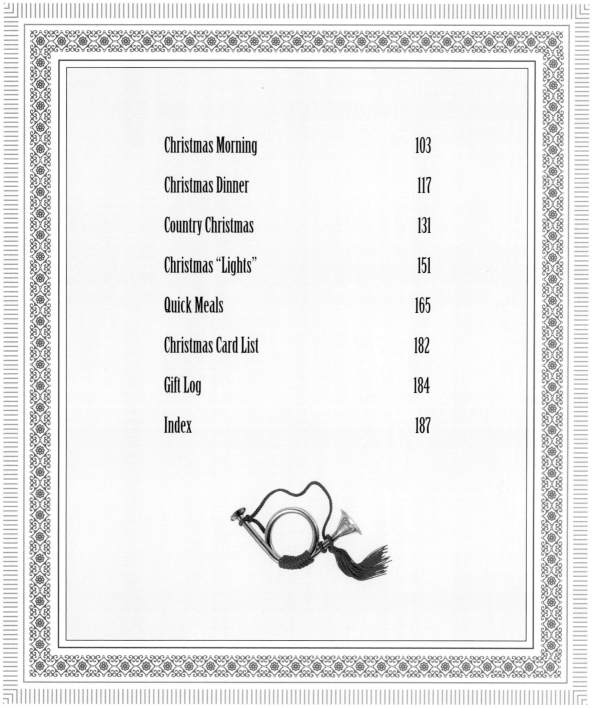

Introduction

Just imagine this: It's a cold winter day and there's a light snow falling. Inside there's a load of activity surrounding a jolly gentleman sitting at his desk and opening sack after sack of mail. You recognize him from his whitish-gray beard and classic-looking hat. Letter after letter is opened and, after each one is carefully read, hearty laughter fills the room.

Right about now you're probably thinking of that jolly bearded fellow from up north who's known for his catchy slogan. Well, you're right—I've just described me, Mr. Food . . . at least that's the way my office staff always described me when I lived and worked in Upstate New York! In those days, my office resembled the scene I just described. And all I have to do to feel the chill of those cold winter days again is close my eyes and picture that scene myself.

Even though there's no snow where I live now, and when I look outside it's pretty likely that I'll see sunshine and palm trees, one thing hasn't changed—reading my Mr. Food mail is still one of my favorite things to do. It's my way of really finding out what my readers and viewers want. And when I get request after request for a certain recipe or topic, I do my best to address it.

Sure, I get lots of requests for desserts and quick-and-easy dinnertime solutions. But last November, December, and January I was amazed by the number of letters I got from people wanting to know how to avoid the holiday food preparation stress. In letter after letter, people practically begged for solutions or new ideas to make that busy holiday time easier and more enjoyable. Sure, many of those letters came from people who already have other Christmas cookbooks—but they told me they were looking for one that was quick, easy, and fun. And they wanted a cookbook with recipes that didn't force them to run all over town looking for fancy ingredients. It had to have no-nonsense instructions and the end results needed to be super dishes that not only tasted great but looked terrific, too.

Well, you asked for it and here it is . . . *A Mr. Food Christmas, Homemade and Hassle-Free*. It's ten chapters filled with all the recipes you'll need to survive and *enjoy* the busiest season of all. I've got some sample menus in here, but don't be afraid to mix and match dishes from different chapters or mix in a few of your classic holiday recipes. And just because this is a Christmas book, don't pack it away with all your Christmas decorations at the end of the season. Use these super recipes all year long—whenever you want to make any day feel like a holiday.

The waiting's over! It's time to sit down and give yourself a well-deserved present. Start by picking out one or two recipes to help you out on those busy preholiday evenings when you need a quick meal so you can move on to other things like addressing cards, cleaning, and shopping. Or maybe start by planning your holiday feast. With my help, you're practically guaranteed a Christmas that's not only homemade and hassle-free, but one where each scrumptious mouthful is full of "OOH IT'S SO GOOD!!®"

ENJOY!

A Moderate Approach

You don't have to give up eating lighter just because the holidays are here. Just follow a few basic steps and you'll be ready to enjoy healthier eating all through the season and beyond. Here are a few ideas to help you substitute lighter ingredients and methods in your everyday cooking. With a little moderation, together we'll enjoy many more seasons of *"OOH IT'S SO GOOD!!®"*

CHICKEN	In most recipes, you can substitute boneless, skinless chicken breasts for whole chicken or parts. Remember that boneless breasts are generally thinner, so they'll cook more quickly than bone-in parts; adjust your cooking times accordingly.
DAIRY	Let's look to our supermarket dairy case for some reduced-fat, low-fat, or fat-free alternatives. For instance, there's low-fat milk for our soups and sauces, instead of heavy cream. (Evaporated skim milk will work, too.)
Cream Cheese	Easy—use light or fat-free cream cheese!
Mozzarella Cheese	Many of the low-fat and part-skim mozzarella cheeses taste just as good as the traditional types. They're perfect alternatives, plus you can also usually cut down on the amount you use. (We can often reduce the amount of cheese we sprinkle on the tops of casseroles without anybody even noticing!)
Parmesan Cheese	Parmesan is an excellent choice when watching fat and calories, since its strong flavor

means that a little goes a long way! (It's the same with Romano cheese.)

Ricotta Cheese For rich taste while still watching fat, in most ricotta recipes you can use half regular ricotta and half light or fat-free ricotta. Or, don't hesitate to use all light or fat-free. The choice is yours.

Sour Cream I often use light versions without missing any flavor, but because sour cream varies widely by brand, I recommend trying several brands until you find the one with the taste and consistency you like best.

Whipped Cream Many desserts call for whipped cream or whipped topping. To watch calories and fat with those, we've got great choices available with reduced-fat and nonfat whipped toppings. You may need to increase the flavoring or sugar a bit, though, depending on the recipe.

DRESSINGS Add a splash of vinegar or citrus juice (lemon, lime, or orange) to dressings or marinades (and vegetables, poultry, and almost anything else, too) in place of some of the traditional oil.

EGGS In many cases, we can replace whole eggs with egg whites. (Two egg whites equal one whole egg.) And, yes, in most recipes, you can go ahead and replace eggs altogether with egg substitute. (It's usually available near the eggs in the refrigerated section of the supermarket.)

However, I don't recommend using egg substitute when coating foods for breading. Breading doesn't stick to it very well.

MAYONNAISE

When it comes to mayonnaise, there are lighter varieties available, too. And when using it in a salad, mix it in just before serving . . . you can usually get by with using less that way. Or sometimes I use a combination of half mayonnaise and half low-fat yogurt. It does the trick, too!

MEATS

- Choose lean cuts of meat and trim away any visible fat before preparing.
- Serve moderate-sized portions, such as 3 to 4 ounces of cooked meat (4 to 6 ounces raw) per adult. (That's about the size of a deck of playing cards.)
- Choose cooking methods like roasting on a rack, broiling, and grilling that allow fat to drip away during cooking.
- Remove the layer of fat that rises to the top of soups, stews, and the pan juices of roasts. Chilling makes this a breeze, so it's even easier to do with dishes that are made ahead and chilled before being reheated. Or, a timesaving tip for removing fat from soups and stews is to simply add a few ice cubes to the warm cooked dish. As soon as the fat sticks to the cubes, remove them, and the fat will come out right along with them!

Ground Beef
and Pork

- Select a very lean blend, preferably with a 90 to 10 ratio of lean meat to fat. (Regular ground beef and pork usually have a 70 to 30 ratio.)
- If browning ground beef or pork before adding it to a recipe, after browning, place it in a strainer and rinse it with warm water, then drain and continue as directed. This should remove most of the excess fat.
- In most recipes, you can replace ground beef or pork with turkey. Keep in mind, though, that ground turkey needs more seasoning than beef or pork.

Sausage

Many markets now offer a variety of lean sausages. This means that there's less fat mixed in with the meat when the sausage is made. Other alternatives to traditional pork or beef sausage are turkey and chicken sausages. Whichever way you go, be sure to read the nutrition label so you know your fat and calorie savings.

NUTS

When a recipe calls for nuts, don't be afraid to cut down the amount. Usually we can cut the amount in half and still get great flavor and texture.

OILS

Select oils such as canola or safflower for frying; they're lower in saturated fat than other types.

SAUCES

Have you seen all the prepared sauces available in the supermarket lately? Not only are there lots of flavors available, but most manufacturers are offering sauces that have less fat and calories, and even ones with less sodium, too. Some of these may be thinner than our "regular" sauces, so you may want to use a bit less of them than normal.

SOUPS Canned soups are a great beginning for sauces and casseroles. If we choose lighter or reduced-fat or reduced-sodium versions, we can sure save calories and cut down on fat and sodium.

How you eat is almost as important as *what* you eat. So follow these basic common-sense eating habits:

- Eat regularly scheduled meals and limit eating between meals. There are two rules of thumb on this: Eat three scheduled meals a day and limit eating between meals *OR* eat five to six light meals throughout the day. But don't do both, and *never* stuff yourself!

- Try not to eat within two hours of bedtime.

- Watch portion sizes! Smaller portions mean fewer calories, so serve yourself only as much food as you think you'll eat. It's okay to leave some on your plate, too.

A Note About Packaged Foods

Packaged food sizes may vary by brand. Generally, the sizes indicated in these recipes are average sizes. If you can't find the exact package size listed in the ingredients, whatever package is closest in size will usually do the trick.

A Note About Serving Sizes

As you go through this book, you'll find lots of different recipes that you'll want to mix and match for your preholiday and holiday meals. The number of servings may vary, so go ahead and adjust the recipes accordingly, keeping in mind that, typically, every guest doesn't eat every dish. They'll have a lot of this and a little of that and maybe none of something else. But if you know that your gang loves potatoes and usually passes on the veggies, then go ahead and adjust your recipe choices and amounts to fit the occasion and the guest list.

Tree Decorating Party

1

I remember some friends telling me the story of how one of their favorite Christmas traditions started many years ago. You see, when they were first married, they could barely afford a Christmas tree, much less any ornaments, lights, and garlands to decorate it. So instead of having a bare Christmas tree, they decided to throw a tree-decorating party.

They invited all their friends and family and asked each person to bring an ornament to hang on their tree. To keep costs to a minimum, they made the invitations themselves and prepared really simple snacks and goodies to serve. And, as the story goes, the party was a huge success. Most people had never heard of this type of get-together and were honored to join the newlyweds in creating their first Christmas tradition.

These many years later, the tradition continues in their family—but it's since been passed down to their children and now to their grandchildren. And each Christmas, when my friends hang the ornaments on their tree, they're reminded of all the special friends and family they have. It's a chance for them to relive so many happy Christmas memories.

Why not try this yourself? Whether you're just beginning to collect ornaments or have so many that you need help unpacking and hanging them all, invite friends and family to share the joy of decorating your Christmas tree. It's nice to kick back and relax together—no fancy clothes or gourmet recipes, just family, good friends, and simple, yummy snacks. What a great way to add the finishing touch of togetherness that makes Christmas so special.

Creamy Pesto Dip

about 2 ½ cups

With all the work that's involved in hosting most parties, it's always nice to have a few dependable shortcut recipes. You know—the ones that take just a few minutes but taste like we spent hours making 'em. This creamy pesto dip really fits the bill! And to save even more time, head to the produce section for some precut carrots, broccoli florets, and other veggies to dip into it. After all, we need all our energy for the decorating job ahead.

   1 cup mayonnaise
   1 cup sour cream
   1 container (7 ounces) pesto sauce
   ½ teaspoon salt
   ¼ teaspoon black pepper

In a medium bowl, combine all the ingredients; mix well. Serve, or cover and chill until ready to serve.

Frosty the Cheese Ball

about 3 cups

Why serve plain old cheese and crackers when we can have a tasty snowman cheese ball on the table? Not only does it make a super-looking centerpiece, but it sure does taste good spread on crunchy crackers!

TIP: It's fun to garnish this with sliced black olives for the eyes and mouth, a baby carrot for the nose, and red bell pepper triangles for buttons, but feel free to use any of your favorite edible delights.

2 packages (8 ounces each) cream cheese, softened
1 container (3 ounces) real bacon bits
1¼ cups finely chopped walnuts
¼ cup mayonnaise
2 scallions, finely chopped
½ cup chopped fresh parsley
1 tablespoon horseradish
¼ teaspoon crushed red pepper

In a large bowl, combine all the ingredients; mix well. Divide the mixture into three balls: one small, one medium, and one large. Arrange the balls on a serving platter in a line to form a snowman lying down. Serve, or cover and chill until ready to serve.

Fiesta Shrimp

about 3 cups

Just like the Spanish Christmas carol and holiday greeting, "Feliz Navidad," this appetizer sure is perfect for wishing guests a Merry Christmas!

1 pound cooked peeled shrimp
1 jar (16 ounces) salsa
½ cup finely chopped fresh cilantro
1 tablespoon lime juice

Reserve a few whole shrimp for garnish, then coarsely chop the remaining shrimp and place in a medium bowl. Add the remaining ingredients; mix well. Cover and chill for at least 1 hour before serving. Garnish with the reserved shrimp.

Tomato and Basil Bruschetta

about 1 dozen slices

What's a holiday party without a few festive touches? I mean, besides the Christmas cookies and colorful decorations on the table, why not make some of the munchies spirited, too—like this tomato and basil bruschetta? It's color-coordinated especially for the holidays!

1 loaf (12 ounces) French bread, cut lengthwise in half
¼ cup olive oil
¼ teaspoon salt
½ cup shredded (not grated) Parmesan cheese, divided
¼ cup chopped fresh basil
1 large tomato, chopped

Preheat the broiler. Place the bread cut side up on a baking sheet. Brush evenly with the olive oil. Sprinkle with the salt, ¼ cup Parmesan cheese, the basil, and tomato. Top with the remaining ¼ cup Parmesan cheese and broil for 4 to 7 minutes, or until the bread is golden. Slice and serve.

Deck the Halls Chili

8 to 10 servings

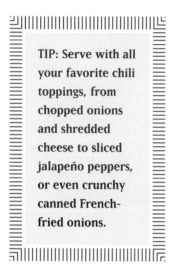

TIP: Serve with all your favorite chili toppings, from chopped onions and shredded cheese to sliced jalapeño peppers, or even crunchy canned French-fried onions.

Depending on where we celebrate the holidays, there's a good chance the temperature will be a bit on the cool side . . . maybe even downright freezing! So why not have a Crock-Pot full of chili to keep spirits up and tummies warm? It's perfect, 'cause the gang can help themselves whenever they get a break from all the decorating.

2½ pounds lean ground beef
1½ pounds hot Italian sausage, casings removed
2 large onions, chopped
2 garlic cloves, minced
2 cans (15½ ounces each) red kidney beans, undrained
1 can (28 ounces) crushed tomatoes
¼ cup chili powder
1 teaspoon ground cumin
1 teaspoon salt
½ teaspoon black pepper

In a soup pot, brown the ground beef, sausage, onions, and garlic over high heat for 20 to 25 minutes, stirring frequently. Add the remaining ingredients; mix well and bring to a boil. Reduce the heat to medium-low and simmer for 30 minutes, stirring occasionally.

Candy Cane Bread Sticks

3 dozen bread sticks

Now we can have two kinds of candy canes on the table—traditional ones and these bread sticks, perfect for dunking in hearty Deck the Halls Chili (page 8). But make no mistake, they're tasty enough to gobble down all by themselves . . . and they're pretty festive, too.

1 package (10 ounces) refrigerated pizza dough
1 tablespoon butter, melted
¼ teaspoon garlic powder
¼ teaspoon salt
1 tablespoon poppy seeds

Preheat the oven to 425°F. Unroll the pizza dough on a work surface. In a small bowl, combine the butter, garlic powder, and salt; mix well, then brush over the dough. Sprinkle with the poppy seeds. Cut the dough crosswise into eighteen ½-inch strips, then make one cut lengthwise, cutting all the strips in half. Twist each strip into a swirled pattern, then form into a candy cane shape and place 1 inch apart on ungreased baking sheets. Bake for 5 to 7 minutes, or until golden around the edges.

TIP: These can also be topped with dried onion flakes or any favorite seasonings.

Holiday Pinwheels

about 64 slices

Since we're all gonna have one hand busy hanging ornaments on the tree, the best food for the occasion is finger food that we can hold in our other hand. Take these pinwheels—they're a combination of the traditional Christmas tastes of cranberries and ham (or turkey), rolled into a handy wrap.

TIP: After cutting these, add a fancy festive toothpick to each and watch them disappear!

1 package (8 ounces) cream cheese, softened
¼ cup raspberry preserves
Eight 10-inch flour tortillas
5 ounces fresh flat-leaf spinach, trimmed
1 pound thinly sliced deli ham or turkey

In a small bowl, combine the cream cheese and raspberry preserves; mix well. Spread over the tortillas and top with the spinach leaves, then the meat slices. Roll up tightly jelly-roll style and wrap each one in a large piece of waxed paper, twisting the ends to seal. Chill for at least 2 hours before serving. Unwrap, cut diagonally into 1-inch slices, and serve.

Crème de Menthe Brownies

12 to 15 bars

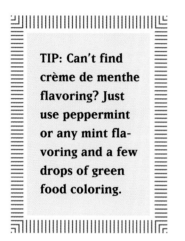

TIP: Can't find crème de menthe flavoring? Just use peppermint or any mint flavoring and a few drops of green food coloring.

Sure, we've all seen those "gourmet" brownies at our favorite bakeries and grocery stores—the rocky road and peanut butter kinds. Well, add these to the list. They're mint brownies that look so elegant your guests will think you bought 'em. But one bite will tell them these are too tasty to be store-bought. Yup, stand up and be proud to say that these are "homemade and hassle-free!"

1 package (19.8 ounces) brownie mix, batter prepared
    according to the package directions
1 container (16 ounces) vanilla frosting
1 tablespoon crème de menthe flavoring (see Tip)
½ cup (3 ounces) semisweet chocolate chips, melted

Bake the brownie batter in a 9" × 13" baking dish according to the package directions. Allow to cool completely. In a medium bowl, combine the frosting and crème de menthe flavoring; mix well. Spread over the brownies. Using a fork, drizzle the melted chocolate in a crisscross pattern over the frosted brownies. Allow the chocolate to set, then cut into bars and serve.

Napoleon Trifle

10 to 12 servings

Whether you make your napoleons from scratch or get 'em from the bakery, there's always the challenge of cutting them without their becoming mush. Well, here's an easy variation that tastes pretty darned close to the original. And it's much simpler to eat, so your guests have more time to trim the tree.

1 package (17¼ ounces) frozen puff pastry, thawed
1 package (4-serving size) instant vanilla pudding and
    pie filling
1½ cups milk
1 container (12 ounces) frozen whipped topping, thawed
    (see Tip)
½ cup chocolate-flavor syrup

Unfold the puff pastry and place each sheet on a baking sheet. Bake according to the package directions until golden. Allow the pastry to cool. In a large bowl, whisk the pudding mix and milk until thickened. Stir in half of the whipped topping until thoroughly mixed. Break the cooled pastry into large pieces and place one third of them in the bottom of a trifle dish or large glass bowl. Spoon half of the pudding mixture over that and drizzle with one third of the chocolate syrup. Repeat the layers, then top with the remaining broken-up pastry, the whipped topping, and the remaining chocolate syrup. Cover and chill for at least 2 hours before serving.

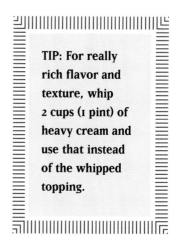

TIP: For really rich flavor and texture, whip 2 cups (1 pint) of heavy cream and use that instead of the whipped topping.

13

Edible Tree Ornaments

about 3 dozen cookies

No Christmas party is complete without a tray of cutout cookies shaped like Christmas trees, gingerbread people, stars, angels, and bells. And the best part about these cookies is that they can be used as ornaments, too. Start by making two batches. Simply punch a hole in the top of the cookies in the first batch (see Tip); those will be used as ornaments. The second batch is for the gang to decorate

Did You Know . . .
the first recorded mention of a Christmas tree was in the diary of Matthew Zahm of Lancaster, Pennsylvania, on December 20, 1821?

and eat at the tree-trimming party. Since everybody can't usually fit around the tree at the same time, it's fun to have something else for them to decorate!

1 cup (2 sticks) butter, softened
¾ cup sugar
2 eggs
1 teaspoon vanilla extract
3½ cups all-purpose flour

In a large bowl, cream the butter and sugar. Add the eggs and vanilla; beat for 1 to 2 minutes, until light and fluffy. Gradually add the flour and beat for 2 minutes, or until well blended. Form the dough into a ball; cover and chill for at least 2 hours. Preheat the oven to 350°F. Divide the dough into two pieces and return one to the refrigerator. On a lightly floured work surface, using a rolling pin, roll the dough to a ¼-inch thickness. Using cookie cutters, cut out assorted Christmas shapes and place on ungreased cookie sheets. Repeat with the remaining dough and bake for 10 to 12 minutes, or until golden around the edges. Remove to a wire rack to cool completely.

TIP: Before baking, use a straw to make a hole at the top of each cookie that you plan to hang up. (That's where you'll thread them with ribbon for hanging on the tree.) Then sprinkle them with colored sugar or sprinkles.

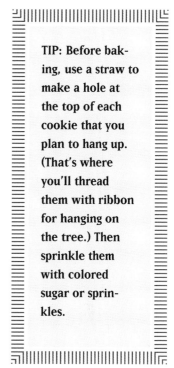

GREAT GO-ALONG:
Frost the cooled cookies with a glaze made of 2 cups confectioners' sugar, 2 tablespoons milk, and red or green food color.

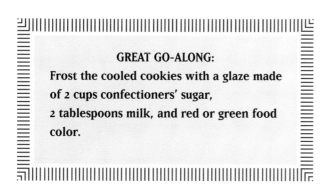

Gingerbread House

1 house

A Christmas tree is only so big, which means not everyone can decorate it at the same time. And there's only so much room at the buffet table, so that leaves a few people looking for something fun to do. Here's a solution—they can build and decorate this easy gingerbread house. And, just like our own homes, this one can be decorated and landscaped according to our personal tastes. Yes, I do mean tastes!

HOUSE

5 cups all-purpose flour
2 teaspoons ground cinnamon
2 teaspoons ground ginger
½ teaspoon ground cloves
½ teaspoon baking soda
½ teaspoon salt
1 cup vegetable shortening
1 cup sugar
½ cup molasses
2 eggs

Using cardboard or waxed paper, cut 1 pattern for each piece shown on page 19. Preheat the oven to 350°F. In a large bowl, combine the flour, cinnamon, ginger, cloves, baking soda, and salt; mix well and set aside. In another

16

large bowl, beat the shortening and sugar until creamy. Add the molasses and eggs; beat until well combined. Slowly stir in the flour mixture until a smooth dough forms. Divide the dough into three balls. Place one ball of dough on the back of a cookie sheet. Using a lightly floured rolling pin, roll out the dough to a ⅛-inch thickness. Using the patterns, use a sharp knife to cut out two front/back pieces; remove any excess dough from around the pieces. Bake for 10 to 12 minutes, or until lightly browned around the edges. Allow to cool slightly, then remove to wire racks to cool completely. Meanwhile, repeat with another dough ball, cutting and baking two side pieces. Repeat with the third dough ball, cutting and baking two roof pieces. Form the scraps into a ball, roll out, and cut and bake one base piece.

TIP: If raw egg whites are used in the icing, don't eat this. It'll be for fun and decoration only.

ICING

3½ cups confectioners' sugar
3 egg whites or equivalent in egg white powder

In a large bowl, beat the confectioners' sugar and egg whites until smooth. Place in a pastry bag with a small tip (or place in a resealable plastic storage bag and cut a tiny piece off a bottom corner of the bag).

18

ASSEMBLY

Place the base flat side down in the center of a large platter or piece of foil-wrapped cardboard. Lay the sides and ends of the gingerbread house flat side down around the base. Pipe icing all around the edges of each piece. Carefully lift and press the edges of the back piece and one side together, sealing with the icing. Lift the front piece

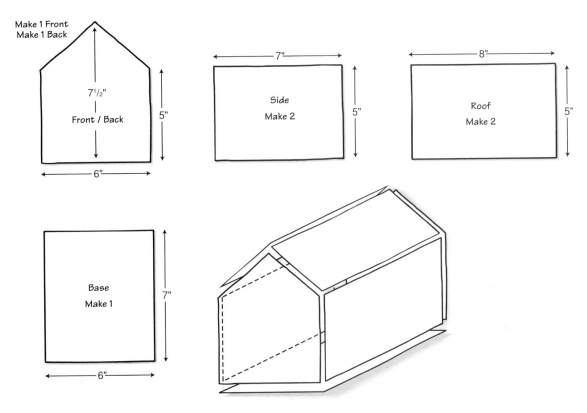

Make 1 Front
Make 1 Back

7½"

Front / Back

5"

6"

7"

Side

Make 2

5"

8"

Roof

Make 2

5"

Base

Make 1

7"

6"

and the remaining side and hold in place until the house is secure; let stand for a few minutes. Add additional icing to strengthen the joints. Place one roof piece in place. Pipe icing along the inside edge of that piece and place the second roof piece in place. Pipe icing along all the seams of the house for extra support and allow to dry. Add frosted mini shredded wheat "shingles" to the roof and a graham cracker "chimney," "windows," and "doors," securing them with icing. Pipe icing "icicles" all around the lower edges of the roof.

Decorate the house and yard with any of the following, using the icing as the glue:

- gumdrops
- hard candies
- M&M's
- marshmallows
- red-hot cinnamon candies
- spearmint leaves (they make great trees!)
- anything else you dream up!

Holiday Punches

A big bowl of punch is a necessity at any Christmas bash, and it sure makes a fancy centerpiece when it's served in a decorative bowl with fruit slices floating on top. These are punches that everybody can have—including the kiddies at the party and adults who prefer to avoid spirits. It's nice to have a choice of punches—a thick and creamy type and a fizzy fruit variety—so here they are!

Did You Know . . .
the word *nog* is an Old English term for ale?

Pineapple Nog

6 to 8 servings

4 cups (2 pints) heavy cream, well chilled
1 cup egg substitute (see Tip)
¾ cup sugar
1½ cups pineapple juice, chilled

TIP: For safety's sake, I use egg substitute instead of real fresh eggs.

In a punch bowl, combine the heavy cream, egg substitute, and sugar, stirring until the sugar dissolves. Add the pineapple juice and stir until well blended. Serve immediately, or chill until ready to serve.

CITRUS TWIST PUNCH

21 to 28 servings

TIP: For a really festive look, float a few orange, lemon, and/or lime slices on the top of the punch.

½ gallon orange juice, chilled
½ gallon lemonade, chilled
1 container (32 ounces) cranberry-raspberry juice, chilled
1 liter ginger ale, chilled
1 quart rainbow sherbet

In a punch bowl, combine the orange juice, lemonade, and cranberry-raspberry juice; stir until well mixed. Add the ginger ale and sherbet. Serve immediately.

Open House Welcomes

Every December, it seems like our mailboxes just overflow with all kinds of colorful mail. There are Christmas cards from friends and family, holiday catalogs advertising toys and other fun items for our gift lists, and invitations to parties and open houses. Sure, we like reading our cards and checking out the sales and gift ideas, but the invitations are probably the most welcome, 'cause we know what they mean—friends, fun, and food!

At holiday open houses, you can expect buffet tables covered with loads of tasty treats, fizzy punches, and, of course, everybody's favorite: sweets! It's a wonder that people can find the time to have open houses at such a busy time of year. And how do they do it? They know a few shortcuts, of course! Well, I've assembled a few of my own over the years, so whether you're hosting an open house this Christmas or need to take an easy dish to somebody else's party, this chapter is for you!

I hope my ideas inspire you to open your heart and home this holiday season. Isn't that what the holidays are all about—getting together with friends and family and sharing fun times?

Pistachio-Stuffed Mushrooms

16 mushrooms

Stuffed mushrooms are probably one of the most popular appetizers served at holiday parties. It seems everyone has their own version, which, of course, are "the only way to make them." Often they're stuffed with a mixture of sausage or chopped mushrooms and bread crumbs, so I decided to share a slightly different version. When I bring these to parties, they're an instant success. So go ahead and try 'em. . . . I bet these'll become "the only ones to make!"

16 large mushrooms (about 1 pound)
½ small onion, minced
¼ cup pistachios, coarsely chopped
6 tablespoons (¾ stick) butter
⅓ cup plain bread crumbs
2 tablespoons chopped fresh parsley
¼ teaspoon salt
¼ teaspoon black pepper

Preheat the oven to 350°F. Remove the mushroom stems from the caps; finely chop the stems. In a large skillet, sauté the chopped mushroom stems, the onion, and pistachios in the butter over medium heat until the stems and onion are tender. Remove from the heat and stir in the remaining ingredients; mix well. Stuff each mushroom cap and place on a large rimmed baking sheet. Bake for 20 to 25 minutes, or until the mushrooms are tender.

TIP: You might want to sprinkle these with additional chopped pistachios for an even nuttier taste.

Roasted Pepper Dip

about 1½ cups

Say good-bye to ordinary dips and bring on this one that's "new and improved"!

1 package (8 ounces) cream cheese, softened
1 jar (7¼ ounces) roasted red peppers, drained
½ teaspoon ground red pepper
½ teaspoon salt

In a blender, blend all the ingredients on high speed for 1 to 2 minutes, or until well combined and smooth. Serve, or cover and chill; allow to soften slightly before serving.

Cocktail Bundles

about 4 dozen bundles

Looking for a little something to take along to somebody else's get-together? How about these? They're a twist on pigs in a blanket, but better, 'cause we don't have to spend time rolling out dough and pinching every one closed. And since this has a honey-mustard tang that everybody loves, it's gonna make you a very welcome guest!

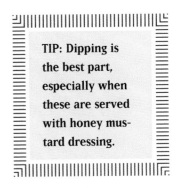

TIP: Dipping is the best part, especially when these are served with honey mustard dressing.

⅓ cup honey mustard
Eight 8-inch flour tortillas
1 package (16 ounces) cocktail franks
Nonstick cooking spray

Preheat the oven to 350°F. Spread the honey mustard evenly over the tortillas. Cut each tortilla into six even strips. Roll up a cocktail frank in each strip and place seam side down on a baking sheet. Lightly coat the tortillas with nonstick cooking spray and bake for 12 to 15 minutes, or until heated through and golden.

Swedish Meatballs

about 4 dozen meatballs

TIP: No toothpicks? No problem. Pretzel sticks work well, too—and they're an edible bonus!

No matter how many "fancy, schmancy" hors d'oeuvres and elegant platters we put out, it seems like the cocktail meatballs always get the most attention. It's hard to get your toothpick close to the serving bowl when everybody's swarming around it, but, believe me, these are worth the wait! Got your toothpick ready?

1½ pounds ground beef
¼ cup plain bread crumbs
1 small onion, finely chopped
1 egg
1½ teaspoons ground cumin
¼ teaspoon salt
½ teaspoon black pepper
1 jar (12 ounces) beef gravy
½ cup sour cream

Preheat the oven to 375°F. Coat two large rimmed baking sheets with nonstick cooking spray. In a large bowl, combine the ground beef, bread crumbs, onion, egg, cumin, salt, and pepper; mix well. Shape into 1-inch balls and place on the baking sheets. Bake for 15 to 20 minutes, or until lightly browned and no pink remains. Meanwhile, in a medium saucepan, combine the gravy and sour cream over medium heat until smooth and warmed through, stirring frequently. Drain the meatballs and add to the gravy mixture, stirring until well coated.

Bourbon Chicken Bites

6 to 8 servings

With all the munching and picking we do at open houses, it's nice to have a few choices of things that aren't filling but are still packed with flavor. It's Christmas, so when you taste these, think about that expression about good things coming "in small packages"!

TIP: To add sparkle to your table, polish your silver chafing dish and use it to serve these tasty nuggets.

2 tablespoons cornstarch

1 teaspoon garlic powder

1 teaspoon ground red pepper

½ teaspoon salt

2 pounds boneless, skinless chicken breasts, cut into 2-inch chunks

¼ cup canola oil

1 cup jalapeño pepper jelly

1 tablespoon light soy sauce

2 tablespoons bourbon

In a medium bowl, combine the cornstarch, garlic powder, ground red pepper, and salt; add the chicken and toss to coat well. Heat the oil in a large skillet over high heat. Add the coated chicken in batches and cook for 6 to 8 minutes, or until golden and no pink remains, stirring frequently. Meanwhile, in a large saucepan, bring the jelly, soy sauce, and bourbon to a boil over medium heat. Cook for 2 to 3 minutes, or until the jelly has melted, stirring constantly. Add the chicken and toss to coat. Serve hot.

Stuffed and Wrapped Brie

1 Brie round

TIP: Serve with thin slices of toasted Italian bread or crackers.

Put away the wrapping paper and Scotch tape, 'cause it's time to wrap a different kind of goodie. This time we're wrapping a sun-dried-tomato-stuffed Brie in puff pastry. And after it's baked, just wait till you watch your happy guests unwrap it!

One 8-ounce Brie cheese round
¼ cup sun-dried tomatoes in oil, drained and chopped
1 sheet frozen puff pastry (from a 17.25-ounce package), thawed

Preheat the oven to 350°F. Slice the Brie round horizontally in half. Remove the top and spread the sun-dried tomatoes over the bottom layer. Replace the top and place in the center of the puff pastry sheet. Bring the corners into the center, completely covering the Brie; pinch the dough firmly to seal. Trim and discard any excess dough and place seam side down on a large rimmed baking sheet. Bake for 30 to 35 minutes, or until the pastry is golden and the Brie is melting. Allow to cool slightly, then serve.

Garlic-Studded Tenderloin

12 to 14 servings

GREAT GO-ALONG: Make a super spread by combining 2 cups mayonnaise with ¼ cup white vinegar, 2 tablespoons chopped fresh tarragon, and 1 teaspoon chopped fresh parsley. Chill it, then serve alongside the tenderloin with crusty rolls and fresh focaccia for elegant make-your-own sandwiches.

Open houses are often at an in-between time—you know, just after lunch or just before dinner. Here's something that's hearty without being too filling. It's a roast tenderloin that's carved really thin. And when it's served with a basket brimming with fresh rolls, you've got the beginning of a buffet that'll work no matter what time you have your party!

 1 whole beef tenderloin (5 to 6 pounds), trimmed
 6 garlic cloves, slivered
 ¾ cup soy sauce
 ¼ cup olive oil
 ½ teaspoon hot pepper sauce
 ¾ cup port wine or other red wine
 1 teaspoon black pepper
 1 teaspoon dried thyme

Make small slits in the tenderloin and insert the garlic slivers; set aside. In a large bowl, combine all the remaining ingredients; mix well. Add the tenderloin, cover, and allow the meat to marinate in the refrigerator for at least 6 hours, or overnight, turning occasionally. Preheat the oven to 425°F. Remove the meat from the marinade and place in a roasting pan; discard the marinade. Roast the meat for 40 to 45 minutes for medium, or to desired doneness. Allow to sit for 20 to 30 minutes before thinly slicing.

Brownie Bonbons

about 3 dozen brownies

Everywhere we look at this time of year we see candy canes. And we can put them on the dessert table, too, but in a different way than you'd think. These festive brownies are so easy, and a super way to use up our broken candy canes, too!

½ cup finely crushed candy canes
1 package (19.8 ounces) brownie mix

Bake the brownies according to the package directions. Place the crushed candy canes in a shallow dish. Remove the brownies from the oven and allow to sit for 5 minutes. While they're still warm, using a spoon or small ice cream scoop, scoop out brownies and roll into 1-inch balls. Immediately roll in the crushed candy canes, coating completely. Allow to cool completely before serving.

TIP: I like to make some of these with traditional candy canes and others with green-and-white ones to get nice color variety for my dessert platters.

Butter Pecan Cheesecake Tarts

2 dozen tarts

Imagine a party where every guest receives his or her own cheesecake! Wow, it sounds too good to be true, but you can make it a yummy reality with this simple recipe.

24 vanilla wafer cookies

¼ cup (½ stick) butter

½ cup chopped pecans

2 packages (8 ounces each) cream cheese, softened

1 can (14 ounces) sweetened condensed milk

2 eggs

2½ teaspoons butter-flavored extract

24 pecan halves

Preheat the oven to 350°F. Line twenty-four muffin cups with paper baking cups and place a vanilla wafer in each. Melt the butter in a medium skillet over medium heat. Add the chopped pecans and sauté for 3 to 5 minutes (be careful not to burn the butter); set aside and allow to cool. In a large bowl, beat the cream cheese and sweetened condensed milk until smooth. Add the eggs and extract and beat until thoroughly combined. Stir in the chopped pecan mixture; mix well and fill each muffin cup three-quarters full. Top each with a pecan half. Bake for 12 to 15 minutes, or until firm. Allow to cool completely, then cover and chill for at least 4 hours before serving.

Layered Cookie Wreath

about 5 dozen cookies

The next time you're invited to a holiday open house, tell your hosts you'll bring a wreath. Imagine how surprised they'll be when you carry in this edible cookie wreath! Like the one hanging on your door, this table wreath's bright and colorful, but it's sweet and crunchy, too. That's *my* kind of wreath!

2 packages (18 ounces each) refrigerated sugar cookie dough
2½ cups confectioners' sugar
3 tablespoons milk
1 teaspoon vanilla extract
¼ teaspoon green food coloring
¼ cup red-hot cinnamon candies

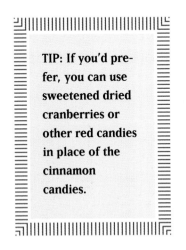

TIP: If you'd prefer, you can use sweetened dried cranberries or other red candies in place of the cinnamon candies.

Roll out the cookie dough according to the package directions for rolled cookies. Using a holly leaf-shaped cookie cutter, cut out the dough and bake the cookies according to the package directions. Allow to cool completely. In a medium bowl, combine the confectioners' sugar, milk, and vanilla; mix well. Stir in the food coloring and mix well. Frost the cookies; place 3 candies in a cluster at one end of each holly leaf. Allow to set completely, then arrange the cookies on a large platter to form a wreath, layering clusters of cookies over each other.

36

"Hole-y" Christmas Tree

24 to 30 servings

The French serve an elegant pastry called *croquembouche* that's a pyramid of miniature cream puffs laced with caramelized sugar. It looks like a fancy golden Christmas tree. The traditional version sure is pretty—and tasty—but it's lots of work. That's why I created this shortcut version that's made in record time, plus it makes a super-looking table centerpiece.

2 cups sugar
1 cup light corn syrup
½ cup water
100 glazed donut holes

> **TIP:** If the sugar glaze becomes too thick, just reheat it until it's pourable again. Feel free to decorate the Christmas tree with assorted candies and top it off with a big colorful ribbon.

In a large saucepan, combine the sugar, corn syrup, and water and bring to a boil over high heat. Cook for 12 to 15 minutes, or until golden, stirring frequently. Remove from the heat. On a large serving plate, form a ring with 14 donut holes. Fill the center of the ring with additional donut holes. Drizzle each donut hole on the plate with the sugar mixture to hold them together. **Be careful when working with the sugar glaze: It is very hot!** Form a ring of 12 donut holes on top of the first ring, then fill the center with additional donut holes; drizzle with the sugar glaze. Continue building smaller rings, using all but one of the donut holes; finish the "tree" by topping with the final donut hole. Allow to set before serving.

> **Did You Know . . .**
> when buying a live Christmas tree it's best to choose one that was locally grown? That's because sometimes a tree shipped from another area may have trouble adjusting to sudden climate changes and may not stay fresh as long as a local one.

Spirited Drinks

What's a party without festive drinks?! These sure will put everybody in the holiday mood, 'cause they're packed with flavor.

Santa's Sangría

16 to 20 servings

1 container (12 ounces) frozen limeade concentrate, thawed

1 container (12 ounces) frozen lemonade concentrate, thawed

1 container (12 ounces) frozen cranberry juice cocktail concentrate, thawed

8 cups Burgundy or other dry red wine

1 liter ginger ale, chilled

32 maraschino cherries

2 limes, washed and thinly sliced

1 orange, washed and thinly sliced

Ice cubes

In a punch bowl, combine the fruit juice concentrates and wine; stir until well combined. Just before serving, add the ginger ale, fruit, and ice.

Peppermint Punch

8 to 10 servings

½ gallon peppermint ice cream, softened
4 cups (1 quart) milk
1 quart vanilla ice cream

In a punch bowl, combine the peppermint ice cream and milk; stir until it reaches a pourable consistency. Using an ice cream scoop, float scoops of the vanilla ice cream in the punch. Serve immediately.

TIP: It's easy to take the minty theme even further by hanging miniature candy canes around the sides of the punch bowl.

Coffee Bar Tips

When we walk down the coffee aisle at the grocery store, it's hard not to be wowed by all the choices. And everybody's got a different favorite! Well, I've got a way to make your whole gang happy—and you won't have to stock up on loads of gourmet flavored mixes to do it. Just keep the basics of coffee, tea, and hot chocolate on hand. Then you can simply give everybody a bunch of these choices for adding zip to their sips:

- A few drops of almost any food flavoring (extracts) can easily be added to hot drinks. Try orange in tea, peppermint in hot chocolate, and butter in warm eggnog. They're really super and they're available in the supermarket spice department.

41

- Combine ¼ teaspoon ground spice with a teaspoon of sugar (or, of course, more if you'd like), and mix it into your hot drink. (In order for the spice to mix in well, it must be mixed with the sugar first.) Try ground cinnamon, nutmeg, or even ginger.

- A fancy choice is to add a bit of liqueur to adults' drinks. Coffee liqueur brings out the rich flavor of coffee, anisette adds a hint of licorice, and a touch of brandy or fruit-flavored liqueur can make coffee a tropical pick-me-up.

- I think some of the best additions to hot beverages are items that add flavor as they melt. For instance, try adding a piece of a chocolate candy bar, some rock candy, or a butterscotch hard candy, and stir until it melts. With every stir comes another burst of pizzazz! Just be sure to melt the candy completely or remove any unmelted pieces before drinking, so that you or your guests won't swallow them whole!

- We even have a large choice of sugars and other sweeteners so we can be creative in sweetening the sips for the lips! Of course, granulated white sugar works fine, but why not offer extra-fine granulated sugar (which melts really easily), brown sugar, maple syrup, or honey. There are some fun sugars on the market, too, like colored granulated "crystal" sugar, coarse "raw" sugar, and good old sugar cubes.

- Oh, yes—don't forget the whipped cream (or prepared whipped topping)! A dollop is just fine.

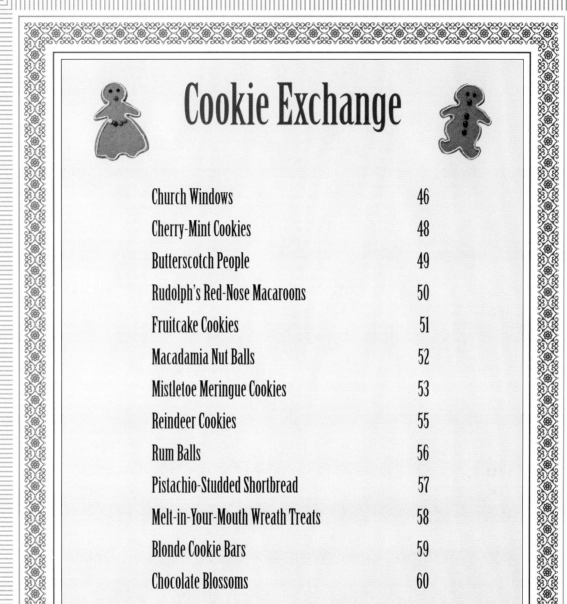

Cookie Exchange

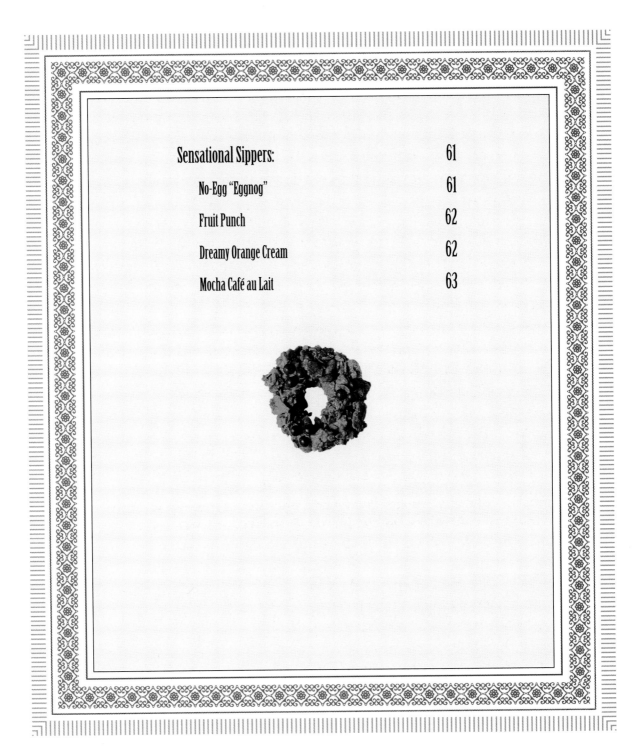

Even though this is a busy time of year, we don't want to give up our traditions. And a favorite one is baking. I bet you'd like some shortcuts to help with your holiday baking, wouldn't you? You know, shortcuts don't have to mean skimping. Uh, uh! When it comes to home-baked goodies, the last thing we want to do is skimp on anything.

So, how can you find the time to make all those different homemade goodies that you want to share at holiday time? Have a cookie exchange! The main idea is that it's easier to bake three, four, or five batches of one type of cookie than one or two batches of many different kinds. So here's how to do that and still end up with an interesting assortment: Find a few friends, neighbors, or relatives who'll each agree to bake several dozen of one or two of their specialties. Make sure everybody chooses something different, then get baking! Have a get-together to exchange some of your cookies for some of everybody else's and fill your pretty tins and boxes with a variety of baked-especially-for-you holiday cookies. And, what do you know, you'll find it was half the work it usually is!

Even if you have plenty of your own favorite cookie recipes, why not take a peek at this chapter? There are bound to be a few new ideas you can use—and maybe even a quick version of one of your classics!

Oh—I almost forgot—when you're doing your exchange, be sure to leave out a few cookies for sampling. Serve the bakers a variety of punches to wash 'em all down and then everybody can go home and check one more thing off their holiday to-do lists. Hooray!

Did You Know . . .
there's a place to call if you wind up with a tray of flat, burned cookies and don't know how it happened? From November 1 through December 24, the trained staff at Land O'Lakes takes calls and answers cookie-related questions at (800) 782-9606 seven days a week, from 8:00 A.M. to 6:00 P.M. CST.

Church Windows

about 4 dozen cookies

There's something magical about stained glass church windows, especially when the sun shines through them. That's why these are perfect for brightening up cookie trays!

½ cup (1 stick) butter, softened
1 package (12 ounces) semisweet chocolate chips
1 teaspoon vanilla extract
1 cup chopped walnuts
1 package (10½ ounces) multicolored miniature
    marshmallows
1 cup sweetened flaked coconut, divided

In a large saucepan, melt the butter and chocolate chips over low heat, stirring constantly. Remove the saucepan from the heat and stir in the vanilla and walnuts. Cool the mixture for about 15 minutes, until cooled but not to the point of hardening. Fold in the marshmallows and stir until well coated. Spoon half of the mixture lengthwise down the center of an 18-inch piece of waxed paper. Shape into a 12" × 2" log and place at one edge of the waxed paper. Sprinkle ½ cup coconut over the remainder of the waxed paper. Roll the log over the coconut, evenly coating the outside of the entire log. Wrap the log tightly in the waxed paper, folding the ends snugly. Repeat with the other half of the marshmallow mixture and the remaining ½ cup coconut. Chill until firm, at least 2 hours, or overnight. Unwrap each log and cut into ½-inch slices.

Cherry-Mint Cookies

about 4 dozen cookies

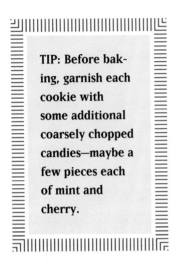

TIP: Before baking, garnish each cookie with some additional coarsely chopped candies—maybe a few pieces each of mint and cherry.

It doesn't get much easier than this. If you're elected to make these, boy, are you lucky! They look so fancy, but really—making these is as easy as baking a cake. (And my cakes are *really* easy!)

1 package (18.5 ounces) devil's food cake mix
⅓ cup vegetable oil
2 eggs
½ cup coarsely chopped Andes® Mint Parfait Thins
½ cup coarsely chopped Andes® Cherry Jubilee Thins

Preheat the oven to 350°F. Coat two cookie sheets with nonstick cooking spray. In a large bowl, beat the cake mix, oil, and eggs until well blended. Stir in the chopped candies; mix well. Drop by teaspoonfuls 2 inches apart onto the cookie sheets. Bake for 9 to 11 minutes, or until firm. Remove to wire racks to cool completely.

Butterscotch People

about 3 dozen cookies

Gingerbread people are a Christmas favorite, but why not try this easy variation? We all love to decorate them, right? With this recipe we save baking time, so there's more time to decorate. Then we can get really creative!

1 package (11 ounces) butterscotch-flavored chips
1 cup (2 sticks) butter
5 cups all-purpose flour
1⅓ cups firmly packed light brown sugar
2 teaspoons baking soda
1 egg
Candies and icing for decoration

Preheat the oven to 375°F. Melt the butterscotch chips and butter in a medium saucepan over low heat until smooth, stirring constantly. Set aside and allow to cool slightly. In a large bowl, combine the flour, brown sugar, baking soda, and egg; mix well. Add the slightly cooled butterscotch mixture and beat until well blended (the dough will be crumbly). Shape into a ball. On a lightly floured cutting board, with a floured rolling pin, roll the dough out to a ¼-inch thickness. Using boy and girl cookie cutters, cut out cookies and place 1 inch apart on ungreased cookie sheets. Decorate as desired with chocolate chips, M&M's, or your favorite candies. For soft cookies, bake for 6 minutes; for crisp cookies, bake for 8 minutes. Cool slightly, then remove to wire racks to cool completely. Ice as desired.

TIP: If you're gonna want to hang these as Christmas ornaments, make a hole at the top of each cookie with a straw before baking. Bake them until crisp; cool, then thread ribbon or string through the holes so they'll be ready for hanging.

Rudolph's Red-Nose Macaroons

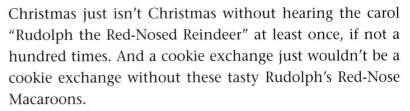

about 3 dozen cookies

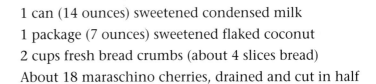

Christmas just isn't Christmas without hearing the carol "Rudolph the Red-Nosed Reindeer" at least once, if not a hundred times. And a cookie exchange just wouldn't be a cookie exchange without these tasty Rudolph's Red-Nose Macaroons.

> **TIP:** For a fancy look, melt ½ cup semisweet chocolate chips and drizzle over the cooled cookies.

1 can (14 ounces) sweetened condensed milk
1 package (7 ounces) sweetened flaked coconut
2 cups fresh bread crumbs (about 4 slices bread)
About 18 maraschino cherries, drained and cut in half

Preheat the oven to 350°F. Coat two cookie sheets with nonstick cooking spray. In a large bowl, combine all the ingredients except the cherries; mix well. Drop by rounded teaspoonfuls 2 inches apart onto the cookie sheets. Press half of a cherry cut side down into the center of each cookie. Bake for 10 to 12 minutes, or until the edges are golden. Allow to cool completely before serving.

Did You Know . . .
Santa loves all the snacks he receives on Christmas Eve? Sure he does! But his favorite is milk and cookies . . . *any* kind of cookies.

Fruitcake Cookies

about 4 dozen cookies

Are you one of those people who turns up your nose at the thought of fruitcake? Trust me, this is no ordinary fruitcake. It's part cake, part cookie, and a whole lot of good taste. And, unlike that other fruitcake—you know, the one that gets passed around from house to house—these cookies are so yummy they might not even make it out of your kitchen!

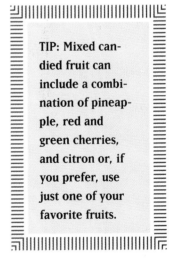

1 pound mixed candied fruit, diced (see Tip)
2 cups chopped pecans
2 cups all-purpose flour, divided
¼ cup (½ stick) butter, softened
1 cup firmly packed light brown sugar
2 eggs
¼ cup milk
1 tablespoon baking powder
½ teaspoon ground cinnamon
½ teaspoon ground nutmeg

Preheat the oven to 325°F. Coat two cookie sheets with nonstick cooking spray. In a large bowl, combine the candied fruit, pecans, and ½ cup flour; toss until evenly coated and set aside. In another large bowl, cream the butter and brown sugar until fluffy. Beat in the eggs and milk. Add the remaining 1½ cups flour, the baking powder, cinnamon, and nutmeg and beat until well blended. Stir in the fruit mixture; mix well. Drop by rounded teaspoonfuls 1 inch apart onto the cookie sheets. Bake for 15 to 18 minutes, or until golden. Remove to a wire rack to cool completely.

TIP: Mixed candied fruit can include a combination of pineapple, red and green cherries, and citron or, if you prefer, use just one of your favorite fruits.

Macadamia Nut Balls

about 4 dozen cookies

You might know these as snowballs, but with the addition of oatmeal and macadamia nuts, they're much, much better. They're richer and crunchier and, well, they're yummier. Be careful if you volunteer to make these for a cookie exchange, 'cause you're guaranteed to eat more than one and you have to have enough left to trade!

2 cups all-purpose flour
1 cup (2 sticks) butter, softened
¾ cup quick-cooking or old-fashioned rolled oats
½ cup granulated sugar
1 teaspoon vanilla extract
1 cup macadamia nuts, coarsely chopped
¾ cup confectioners' sugar

Preheat the oven to 375°F. In a large bowl, beat the flour, butter, oats, granulated sugar, and vanilla until a dough forms. Stir in the nuts; mix well. Roll into 1-inch balls and place 1 inch apart on ungreased cookie sheets. Bake for 12 to 15 minutes, or until light golden on the bottom. Transfer to wire racks and allow to cool for 10 minutes before rolling in the confectioners' sugar, coating completely.

Mistletoe Meringue Cookies

about 2 dozen cookies

Share one of these with your sweetheart and you'll find out how they got their name!

2 egg whites
½ teaspoon vanilla extract
⅓ cup sugar
⅓ cup (2 ounces) mint-flavored semisweet chocolate chips, coarsely chopped

TIP: Have a ball making these with different-flavored chocolate chips, like raspberry. Mmm!

Preheat the oven to 325°F. Coat two cookie sheets with nonstick cooking spray. In a large bowl, beat the egg whites until soft peaks form. Add the vanilla, then gradually beat in the sugar until stiff peaks form. Fold in the chocolate chips. Drop by tablespoonfuls 2 inches apart onto the cookie sheets. Bake for 10 minutes. Turn off the oven and let the cookies sit in the oven for 1 hour. Remove from the oven and allow to cool completely. Serve immediately, or store in an airtight container.

Did You Know . . . as far back as 700 B.C., Britons believed in the healing powers of mistletoe? Nowadays most of us use it to steal a kiss.

Reindeer Cookies

2 dozen cookies

These are sure to be the hit of the cookie exchange 'cause, honestly, they're just so darned cute! They really do look like reindeer. And to really make 'em special, name each one—you know, Dasher, Dancer . . . and don't forget Rudolph!

1 package (18 ounces) refrigerated peanut butter or
   sugar cookie dough
48 small pretzel twists
48 brown M&M's candies
24 red M&M's candies

Place the cookie dough in the freezer for 15 minutes, or until firm. Preheat the oven to 350°F. Cut the dough into 24 slices and place the slices 2 inches apart on large ungreased cookie sheets. Pinch each slice as shown in the photograph. Position 2 pretzels at the top of each slice to form antlers, then create eyes and noses with the M&M's as shown. Bake for 8 to 10 minutes, or until golden. Remove to a wire rack to cool completely.

Rum Balls

about 4 dozen cookies

TIP: Out of rum?
Add bourbon
instead for a new
twist on an old
favorite.

What's a Christmas celebration without rum balls? I mean, they're practically a staple. Rum balls are especially nice served with coffee at an evening get-together. Why, it's like your own version of cordials and coffee. They're extra-easy, too, 'cause they aren't even baked!

1 package (12 ounces) vanilla wafer cookies, finely crushed
1½ cups confectioners' sugar, divided
1 cup finely chopped pecans
½ cup dark rum (see Tip)
3 tablespoons light corn syrup
2 tablespoons unsweetened cocoa

In a medium bowl, combine the crushed cookies, 1 cup confectioners' sugar, the pecans, rum, corn syrup, and cocoa; mix well. Shape into 1-inch balls. Place the remaining ½ cup confectioners' sugar in a shallow dish; roll the balls in the confectioners' sugar, coating completely. Serve immediately, or store in an airtight container.

Pistachio-Studded Shortbread

4 dozen cookies

This is probably one of the most unusual recipes in the collection. Sure, we've all tried regular shortbread or maybe even chocolate shortbread, but have you tried pistachio? Well, once you taste this sweet and salty combination, you'll be hooked.

½ cup pistachio nuts, chopped
1¼ cups all-purpose flour
3 tablespoons sugar
½ cup (1 stick) butter, melted
1 teaspoon almond extract
½ cup (3 ounces) semisweet chocolate chips
½ teaspoon vegetable shortening

Reserve 1 tablespoon chopped nuts. In a medium bowl, combine the remaining nuts, the flour, sugar, melted butter, and almond extract; mix until a dough forms. Roll into a ball and return to bowl; cover and chill for 30 minutes. Preheat the oven to 325°F. On a lightly floured work surface, roll out dough to a 12" × 6" rectangle. Cut into ½" × 3" pieces and place on ungreased cookie sheets 1 inch apart. Bake for 10 to 15 minutes, or until the edges are slightly golden. Remove to wire racks to cool completely. Melt the chocolate chips and shortening in a small saucepan over low heat until smooth, stirring constantly. Drizzle over the shortbread and sprinkle with the reserved nuts. Chill for 15 minutes, or until chocolate has set. Serve immediately, or store in an airtight container.

Melt-in-Your-Mouth Wreath Treats

about 2 dozen wreaths

Is it a cookie or a candy? Well, it's both! Try this fun treat that's a little of this and a little of that . . . and just in time for the holidays.

2 tablespoons vegetable shortening
2 packages (6 ounces each) white baking bars
1½ teaspoons green food coloring
4 cups corn flakes cereal
Red-hot cinnamon candies, for decorating

Line a cookie sheet with waxed paper. In a large saucepan, melt the shortening and baking bars over low heat, stirring constantly. Remove from the heat and stir in the food coloring; mix well. Stir in the corn flakes until evenly coated. Drop by tablespoonfuls onto the cookie sheet. Shape into wreaths by placing your finger in the center of each spoonful and forming a circle. Decorate with the candies. Chill for 30 minutes, or until firm. Serve immediately, or store in an airtight container.

Blonde Cookie Bars

15 to 18 bars

When I first made these for my staff, you should have heard the "ooh"s and "aah"s. I've got a bunch of chocolate lovers working with me, and they still loved the taste of these. In fact, they said these cookies tasted so good we shouldn't just make 'em at Christmastime. I'm sure you'll agree that this is an all-year-round recipe.

2 cups firmly packed light brown sugar
⅔ cup vegetable shortening
2 eggs
2 tablespoons vanilla extract
2 tablespoons water
2 cups all-purpose flour
1 teaspoon baking powder
¼ teaspoon baking soda
1 teaspoon salt
1 cup finely chopped walnuts
½ cup (3 ounces) semisweet chocolate chips, melted

Preheat the oven to 350°F. Coat a 9" × 13" baking dish with nonstick cooking spray. In a large bowl, combine the brown sugar, shortening, eggs, vanilla, and water; mix well. Add the flour, baking powder, baking soda, and salt; mix well. Add the walnuts and stir until well combined. Spread the batter into the baking dish and bake for 30 to 35 minutes, or until a wooden toothpick inserted in the center comes out clean. Allow to cool slightly, then drizzle with the melted chocolate. Allow to cool completely. Cut into bars.

Chocolate Blossoms

about 2 dozen cookies

Around Christmastime there isn't too much blossoming—not outside, anyway. But in our ovens . . . well, that's another story! You'll see.

½ cup unsweetened cocoa
¼ cup (½ stick) butter, melted
1 cup all-purpose flour, divided
1 cup granulated sugar
2 eggs
1 teaspoon vanilla extract
1 teaspoon baking soda
¼ teaspoon salt
¼ cup chopped almonds
¼ cup confectioners' sugar

TIP: I place the confectioners' sugar in a shallow pie plate and roll each cookie in it until it's completely covered.

In a large bowl, stir the cocoa into the melted butter. Cool slightly, then stir in ½ cup flour, the granulated sugar, eggs, vanilla, baking soda, and salt. Beat until well blended. Stir in the remaining ½ cup flour and the almonds until blended. Cover and chill the dough until firm, at least 3 hours, or overnight. Preheat the oven to 300°F. Coat two cookie sheets with nonstick cooking spray. Shape the dough into 1-inch balls and roll each ball in the confectioners' sugar (see Tip). Place the balls 3 inches apart on the cookie sheets. Bake for 10 to 12 minutes, or until the cookies are firm when lightly touched and the tops have "blossomed" (cracked). Immediately remove from the cookie sheets and cool completely on a wire rack.

60

Sensational Sippers

Munching on all these cookies will certainly work up a thirst! So here are some sippers that'll take care of that—and there's something for every taste, from a creamy no-egg eggnog to a fizzy fruit punch. And a favorite cookie partner—coffee . . . except this one's got a chocolate twist. Okay, it's time to sip away and enjoy all that home-baked goodness.

No-Egg "Eggnog"

4 to 6 servings

5½ cups milk
1 package (4-serving size) instant vanilla pudding and pie filling
4 teaspoons rum extract
¾ teaspoon ground nutmeg, divided
2 cups (1 pint) heavy cream
2 tablespoons confectioners' sugar

In a punch bowl, combine the milk and pudding mix; mix well. Add the rum extract and ½ teaspoon nutmeg; mix well and set aside. In a medium bowl, beat the heavy cream and confectioners' sugar until stiff peaks form. Add half of the whipped cream mixture to the milk mixture; stir until well blended. Dollop the remaining whipped cream mixture over the top and sprinkle with the remaining ¼ teaspoon nutmeg. Serve immediately.

Fruit Punch

10 to 12 servings

1 container (32 ounces) cranberry juice cocktail, chilled
2 cups pineapple juice, chilled
1 container (6 ounces) frozen orange juice concentrate
1 container (6 ounces) frozen lemonade concentrate
1 liter ginger ale, chilled
4 cups ice

In a punch bowl, combine the cranberry juice, pineapple juice, orange juice and lemonade concentrates until well mixed and the concentrates are melted. Add the ginger ale and ice; mix well and serve immediately.

Dreamy Orange Cream

6 to 8 servings

TIP: For a festive look, add some orange slices as a garnish.

1 container (12 ounces) frozen orange juice concentrate
2 cups (1 pint) heavy cream
¼ cup firmly packed light brown sugar
¼ teaspoon ground cinnamon
2 cans (12 ounces each) ginger ale, chilled

In a punch bowl or large pitcher, combine all the ingredients except the ginger ale; stir until the orange juice concentrate has melted. Add the ginger ale; mix well and serve. If not serving immediately, refrigerate and add the ginger ale just before serving.

Mocha Café au Lait

6 to 8 servings

4 cups (1 quart) milk
2 cups (1 pint) heavy cream
½ cup chocolate flavor syrup
3 tablespoons instant coffee granules

In a large saucepan, combine all the ingredients; mix well. Cook over medium heat for 8 to 10 minutes, or until the mixture is steaming and bubbly, stirring constantly. Serve immediately.

To Aunt Patty
From Morgan

To Grand
From

Gifts from Your Kitchen

Some people might say that their favorite part of Christmas is the gifts. Sure, we all like receiving presents, but the best part for me is *giving* gifts.

It's usually pretty easy to know what to give the special people in our lives, like our mates, children, and grandchildren. But there are always some "hard to buy for" people on our lists—you know, those people who seem to have everything they need or the people we don't know too well, like our mail carrier, hairdresser, newspaper delivery person, and teachers.

Some people have a drawer or box at home that they keep filled with little just-in-case gifts, like stationery, perfumed sachets, and other miscellaneous items. But if those types of things aren't quite right, what's a gift giver to do? Relax, that's what, 'cause I've got some tasty ideas for the perfect gifts. Now get to work on making these no-fuss sweet recipes to share a unique gift of yourself. They're gifts from the heart for the tummy. What could be better?!

Holly Fudge

about 3 dozen squares

Most people think of fudge as traditionally being made with chocolate, right? But one bite of this fudge and you'll forget tradition. It's rich and creamy, and the red and green candied cherries add that little Christmas touch we're always looking for. Better make two batches, though, 'cause once the gang gets ahold of it, they'll surely eat the whole pan and then there won't be any left for gift-giving!

1 cup granulated sugar
½ cup (1 stick) butter
½ cup heavy cream
⅛ teaspoon salt
2 cups confectioners' sugar
1 teaspoon vanilla extract
1 cup red and green candied cherries, chopped

TIP: If you prefer, leave out the candied cherries and you'll have a great vanilla fudge.

Coat an 8-inch square baking dish with nonstick cooking spray. In a large saucepan, bring the granulated sugar, butter, heavy cream, and salt to a boil over medium heat, stirring frequently. Allow to boil for 5 minutes, stirring constantly. Remove from the heat and slowly add the confectioners' sugar and vanilla, stirring until smooth and well combined. Stir in the cherries until evenly distributed. Spoon into the baking dish and chill for 1 hour, or until firm. Cut into squares and serve, or store in an airtight container.

Cherry Cordials

about 2 1/2 dozen cherries

Take a look around the grocery store or candy shop at Christmastime and you're sure to see boxes and boxes of chocolate-covered cherries. Sure, anybody can pick up a box of 'em as a last-minute gift, but what if I told you I had an easy recipe to make your own—and it's tastier than the rest? Here it is, and arranged on a pretty plate, these cherries sure do make a super-looking gift!

2½ cups confectioners' sugar

¼ cup (½ stick) butter, softened

2 tablespoons milk

1 jar (10 ounces) stemmed maraschino cherries, well drained

1 package (11½ ounces) milk chocolate chips

1 tablespoon vegetable shortening

TIP: These can also be covered in white or semi-sweet chocolate and, for an added touch, after dipping them in chocolate, you can drizzle them with a different chocolate.

Line a baking sheet with waxed paper. In a small bowl, combine the confectioners' sugar, butter, and milk; mix until a stiff mixture forms. Pull off small pieces of the mixture and shape them evenly around each cherry; place on the baking sheet. Freeze for 15 minutes, or until firm. In a small saucepan, melt the chocolate chips and shortening over low heat until smooth, stirring frequently. Remove the coated cherries from the freezer and dip each into the chocolate mixture, coating completely. Return to the baking sheet and chill for 1 hour, or until the chocolate is firm. Serve, or cover and chill until ready to serve.

Peppermint Pretzels

about 2 dozen pretzels

A few years ago, chocolate-covered pretzels hit the scene and in no time they caught on in a big way. Wait till you try these that you can make yourself—they're out of this world! When you need a last-minute gift, it's simple enough to whip up a batch or two of these and wrap them in a colorful Christmas box with pretty ribbons and bows.

1 package (11 ounces) white chocolate chips
1 package (10 ounces) pretzel rods
1½ cups crushed candy canes or peppermint candies

Line two baking sheets with waxed paper. Melt the chips in a small saucepan over low heat until smooth, stirring frequently (do not overheat). Remove from the heat. Holding the top of a pretzel rod, spoon and spread the melted chocolate over the bottom two thirds of the pretzel, allowing any excess chocolate to drip off the pretzel back into the pan. Sprinkle the chocolate with some crushed candy. Place on the baking sheet and repeat with the remaining pretzels. Chill for 10 minutes, or until the chocolate has set. Store at room temperature in an airtight container.

> **Did You Know . . .**
> the first Christmas cards were sent in 1843 by a British businessman to one thousand of his friends and acquaintances? Today, over two billion Christmas cards are exchanged annually!

> TIP: Use different-colored candy canes to create a variety of festive peppermint pretzels.

Chocolate Fruitcake

12 to 16 servings

TIP: Want to fancy this up? Top it with a red or green glaze made by mixing 1 cup confectioners' sugar with 2 tablespoons of either the red or green cherry liquid. For a white glaze, just use confectioners' sugar and 2 tablespoons water or milk. And for an even simpler topping, lightly dust the cake with confectioners' sugar.

We've all heard the story that there's really only one fruitcake in the whole world and it keeps getting passed from person to person. Well, this proves that there's more than one fruitcake. And it happens to be much tastier than traditional fruitcake, too, 'cause it starts with a devil's food cake mix and is packed with nuts, fruit, chocolate, and loads of flavor. I'd better give you fair warning—this one's addicting.

1 package (18.25 ounces) devil's food cake mix
⅓ cup water
1 cup sour cream
3 eggs
1 jar (10 ounces) red maraschino cherries, drained and cut in half
1 jar (6 ounces) green maraschino cherries, drained and cut in half
1 cup (6 ounces) candied pineapple chunks, chopped
2 cups chopped pecans
1 cup (6 ounces) semisweet chocolate chips

Preheat the oven to 350°F. Coat a 10-inch Bundt or tube pan with nonstick cooking spray. In a large bowl, beat the cake mix, water, sour cream, and eggs until well combined. Stir in the remaining ingredients until well mixed. Pour into the prepared pan and bake for 50 to 60 minutes, or until a wooden toothpick inserted in the center comes out clean. Allow to cool for 15 minutes, then invert onto a wire rack to cool completely.

Caramel-Covered Pears

4 servings

We've all seen those fancy chocolate-dipped apples loaded with nuts and caramel topping. In fact, I bet many of you have given them as special gifts. There's one problem—we pay those fancy prices! So why not try this easy variation at home? They're just as tasty and just as fancy-looking, but a whole lot easier on our pocketbooks. (And, yes, you can make this with apples if you prefer.)

1 package (14 ounces) caramels, unwrapped
1 tablespoon water
4 ripe pears with stems
1 cup (6 ounces) semisweet chocolate chips
1 cup finely chopped dry-roasted peanuts

TIP: Wrap each pear in clear cellophane and tie with a ribbon. Place them in a basket for a gift that won't soon be forgotten!

Line a baking sheet with waxed paper and coat with nonstick cooking spray. In a medium saucepan, combine the caramels and water over low heat until melted and smooth, stirring constantly. Remove from the heat. Holding each pear by its stem over the saucepan, spoon the caramel mixture over it, coating completely. Place the coated pears on the baking sheet and chill for 1 hour. Melt the chocolate chips and spoon the chocolate over the caramel-covered pears, then immediately sprinkle with the nuts. Chill for about 30 minutes, or until set. Serve, or cover and keep chilled until ready to serve.

Did You Know . . . there are lots of unique and inexpensive Christmas gift ideas? How about giving homemade coupons for things like baby-sitting, car washes, and gourmet meals?

Crispy Snowman Treats

5 treats

There are tons of parties during the Christmas season, so when you need to bring something with you, why not be different and take along a snowman? No, not a snowman made of snow . . . that kind melts. Make an edible snowman! All the "Oh, it's so cute. Why didn't I think of that?" will be music to your ears.

3 tablespoons butter
1 package (10 ounces) marshmallows (about 40)
6 cups crispy rice cereal
5 round red peppermint candies
8 red jelly beans
10 semisweet chocolate chips
25 miniature semisweet chocolate chips
1 fruit roll-up, cut into ¾-inch strips
15 red-hot cinnamon candies
10 pretzel sticks

TIP: Coat your hands with non-stick cooking spray to keep the marshmallow mixture from sticking to them when forming the cereal balls.

Line a baking sheet with waxed paper and coat with nonstick cooking spray. Melt the butter in a soup pot over low heat. Add the marshmallows and stir until melted. Remove from the heat and add the cereal; stir until completely coated. Using a ¾-cup measure of the mixture for each, form five balls and place on the baking sheet. Using a ⅓-cup measure for each, form five more balls. Place the smaller balls on top of the larger ones, forming snowmen. Decorate with the candies, chips, and pretzels as shown. Serve, or cover loosely with plastic wrap until ready to serve.

Peppermint-Twist Mints

about 3 dozen mints

TIP: For colored mints, use food coloring to color the dough. You might even want to make each piece a different color and twist two colors together.

No, this isn't a Christmas carol by Chubby Checker, it's a melt-in-your-mouth butter mint. It's a perfect gift, especially when placed on an elegant candy dish and wrapped with pretty tissue paper. What better way to say, "Happy Holidays"?

3 cups confectioners' sugar
4 ounces cream cheese, softened
1 teaspoon peppermint extract

Line a baking sheet with waxed paper. In a large bowl, beat all the ingredients until crumbly. Knead until the dough is smooth, then divide into four balls. Roll each ball into an 18-inch-long rope. Twist together two ropes at a time and cut into 1-inch pieces. Place on the baking sheet, cover loosely, and allow to dry overnight.

Chocolate-Almond Apricots

about 4 dozen apricots

Boxes of chocolate-dipped dried fruits are pretty popular holiday gifts, and what better way to show how much you care than to make some yourself? These are better than all the rest 'cause they're dipped in a perfect combination of chocolate and caramel. You might even want to use an assortment of fruit to make this an extra-special gift.

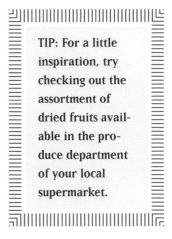

TIP: For a little inspiration, try checking out the assortment of dried fruits available in the produce department of your local supermarket.

> 1 package (6 ounces) chocolate-covered caramels, such as Riesen® Chocolate Chew
> 1 tablespoon water
> ¾ cup chopped almonds, lightly toasted
> 1 package (12 ounces) dried apricots

Line a baking sheet with waxed paper. In a small saucepan, combine the chocolate-covered caramels and water over low heat until melted and smooth, stirring frequently. Place the toasted almonds in a small bowl. Dip each apricot halfway into the chocolate mixture and then into the toasted almonds. Place on the baking sheet and chill for 5 to 10 minutes, or until firm. Store in an airtight container in a cool dry place. Do not refrigerate.

Raspberry Chocolate Truffles

about 2 dozen truffles

TIP: Using a
medium grater,
grate the baking
bar into fine
strands.

To a true chocoholic, there's no better gift than a box of their favorite confections. So if you want to see some genuine smiles, try surprising your favorite chocolate lover with a box filled with these hassle-free truffles.

½ cup evaporated milk
¼ cup sugar
1 package (10 ounces) raspberry-flavored semisweet choco-
    late chips
One 2-ounce white chocolate baking bar, grated (see Tip)

Did You Know . . .
shipping candies requires extra care? Start by using a cardboard box and padding it with newspaper. Wrap the candies carefully in freezer bags. Tape the box well and be sure to clearly mark "Perishable" and "Fragile" on the outside.

In a small saucepan, combine the evaporated milk and sugar over medium heat and cook until the mixture comes to a rolling boil. Boil for 3 minutes, stirring constantly. Remove from the heat and add the chips; stir until melted and the mixture is smooth. Pour into a bowl, cover, and chill for 1 hour, or until the mixture is cool but not firm. Line a baking sheet with waxed paper. Shape the chocolate mixture into 1-inch balls, then roll in the grated white chocolate until evenly coated. Place on the baking sheet, cover loosely, and chill for 1 hour, or until firm. Store in an airtight container in a cool dry place. Do not refrigerate.

Lemon Curd

about 3 ½ cups

Sure, jams, jellies, and preserves used to be an old standby gift, but they haven't been popular in recent years since everybody thinks they take so long to make. Well, not now! Let's try a new flavor and a new method. The name of this lemon-flavored spread may throw you, but go for it, 'cause the taste is anything but ordinary.

2 cups sugar
1 cup (2 sticks) butter
⅔ cup fresh lemon juice
2 tablespoons grated lemon peel
4 eggs, beaten

In a medium saucepan, combine all the ingredients except the eggs over low heat and cook for 5 minutes, or until the butter has melted. Slowly whisk the eggs into the mixture and cook for 12 to 15 minutes, or until the lemon curd is thick enough to coat a spoon, stirring occasionally; do not boil. Place in clean jars or a bowl, cover, and chill for at least 2 hours, or until cool, before serving. Store in the refrigerator.

TIP: If you want to store and give this in canning jars, cover the top of each with a circle of cloth and tie with a ribbon; it makes such a pretty gift! Lemon curd can be used as a filling for cakes or cookies or simply as a toast spread. I bet you'll come up with a few more yummy uses for it, too!

Triple-Chocolate Biscotti

about 4 dozen biscotti

Biscotti have become a staple at all the trendy coffee shops—and it's easy to see why! They're so crunchy and flavorful, they're perfect for dunking in our favorite steaming drinks. Well, I've come up with this easy version that you can make at home for a fraction of the cost of the store-bought ones. They're just right for Christmas cookie platters and gift-giving, and for any time you want something comforting and special to serve with your hot drinks.

2½ cups all-purpose flour
2 cups sugar
¾ cup unsweetened cocoa
1 teaspoon baking soda
½ teaspoon salt
5 eggs
1 teaspoon vanilla extract
1 package (11½ ounces) milk chocolate chips
½ cup white chocolate chips
2 teaspoons vegetable shortening

Preheat the oven to 350°F. Coat two rimmed baking sheets with nonstick cooking spray. In a large bowl, combine the flour, sugar, cocoa, baking soda, salt, eggs, and vanilla; mix well (the dough will be thick and sticky). Stir in the milk chocolate chips. Place half of the dough on each baking sheet. Form each dough into a slightly rounded 4" × 12" loaf about ¾ inch high. Bake for 30 minutes; remove from the oven. Reduce the heat to 325°F. Allow to cool for 5 to 10 minutes, then cut into ½-inch-thick slices. Place the slices cut side down on the baking sheets and bake for 15 more minutes. Turn the cookies over and bake for another 15 minutes, or until very crisp. Allow to cool completely. In a small saucepan, combine the white chocolate chips and the shortening and melt over low heat, stirring constantly. Drizzle over one side of the biscotti and allow to cool until the drizzle is firm. Serve immediately, or store in an airtight container.

Doggie Bone Treats

about 1 dozen biscuits

Let's not forget our favorite furry friend this holiday season. We don't want poor Max or Buddy to feel left out when we're tearing open those holiday packages. Well, this year he won't, not when he gets one, too. It's just one more way to show some TLC.

    1 cup all-purpose flour
    1 cup whole-wheat flour
    ½ cup wheat germ
    ½ cup powdered milk
    3 tablespoons vegetable shortening
    1 teaspoon brown sugar
    ½ teaspoon salt
    ⅓ cup water
    1 teaspoon green food coloring
    1 egg
    1 teaspoon chopped fresh mint, optional

Preheat the oven to 350°F. Coat a cookie sheet with nonstick cooking spray. In a large bowl, combine both flours, the wheat germ, powdered milk, shortening, brown sugar, and salt; mix until crumbly. In a small bowl, combine the water and food coloring; mix well. Add to the flour mixture, along with the egg and mint, if desired; mix well. On a lightly floured surface, knead the dough until smooth. Using a rolling pin, roll to a ½-inch thickness. Using a wreath- or dog-bone-shaped cookie cutter or a knife, cut out biscuits. Place the biscuits on the cookie sheet and bake for 25 to 30 minutes, or until browned around the edges. Remove to a wire rack to cool completely.

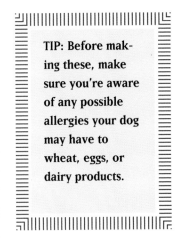

TIP: Before making these, make sure you're aware of any possible allergies your dog may have to wheat, eggs, or dairy products.

The Night Before Christmas

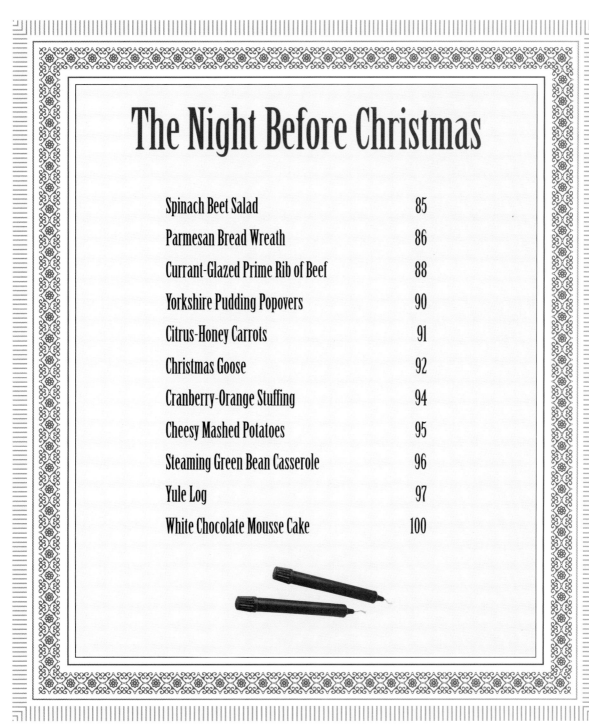

It's finally here! The night everyone's been waiting for—Christmas Eve. The tree's decorated, tiny lights are twinkling, and the sound of Bing Crosby singing "White Christmas" fills the house. There are piles of brightly wrapped presents sitting under the tree and a bunch of excited kids are anxious for Santa Claus to arrive with more!

Then there's the food! For many, it's a tradition to have a houseful of company for Christmas Eve dinner. Depending on your ethnic and family background, that dinner may include anything from ham or turkey with chestnut stuffing to ravioli, stuffed artichokes, and seafood.

Whatever your family's traditions are, it's always nice to add new ones. And I bet you'll find some recipes here to help you do just that.

You know, no matter what we serve on Christmas Eve, one thing's for sure: It's a time for us all to be thankful for what we have and to wish for there to be plenty of food in every home at holiday time and all throughout the year.

Spinach Beet Salad

4 to 6 servings

Some people may wrinkle their noses if spinach or beets are set down in front of 'em. The kids might even say they're "yucky." Trust me, there's nothing yucky about this salad. It's got a nice creamy taste, but it's crunchy, too. Why, it tastes so good, it's a present all by itself!

¼ cup mayonnaise
2 tablespoons sour cream
1 tablespoon fresh lemon juice
Grated peel of ½ lemon
¼ teaspoon salt
¼ teaspoon black pepper
1 package (10 ounces) fresh spinach, trimmed
1 can (15 ounces) julienne-sliced beets, drained
2 tablespoons real bacon bits

> **TIP: If not serving this immediately, prepare the dressing mixture in advance and keep it chilled until ready to toss, top, and serve.**

In a large bowl, combine the mayonnaise, sour cream, lemon juice, lemon peel, salt, and pepper; mix well. Add the spinach and toss until well coated. Place in a serving bowl or on individual salad plates and top with the beets and bacon bits. Serve immediately.

Parmesan Bread Wreath

1 dozen rolls

TIP: If you want, sprinkle a little extra grated Parmesan cheese on top just before serving.

When it comes to Christmas Eve, the more festive the table, the better. Believe it or not, different dinner courses can be turned into Christmas decorations. Take this edible wreath—one glimpse of it and you'll have the entire table humming "It's Beginning to Look a Lot Like Christmas."

1 loaf (1 pound) frozen bread dough, thawed slightly
½ cup (1 stick) butter, softened
1 jar (2 ounces) pimientos, drained and finely chopped
3 tablespoons grated Parmesan cheese
2 tablespoons chopped fresh parsley
¼ teaspoon onion powder

GREAT GO-ALONG: You might want to form the remaining butter mixture into a log on a piece of plastic wrap and freeze it while the bread finishes baking. Then you can slice the log into butter rounds for serving with the warm bread.

Coat a baking sheet with nonstick cooking spray. Cut the bread dough into twelve equal slices and place in a circle, with the slices slightly overlapping, on the baking sheet. Coat lightly with nonstick cooking spray, cover with plastic wrap, and allow to rise for 1 hour, or until doubled in size. Preheat the oven to 400°F. Remove the plastic wrap and bake the wreath for 18 to 20 minutes, or until lightly browned. Meanwhile, in a small bowl, combine the remaining ingredients; mix well. Remove the wreath from the oven and spread some of the butter mixture evenly over the top; reserve the remaining butter mixture. Return the wreath to the oven and bake for 3 to 4 minutes, or until golden. Serve with the remaining butter mixture on the side.

Currant-Glazed Prime Rib of Beef

6 to 8 servings

There's no holding back when it comes to making Christmas Eve dinner. We go all out, and what better way to go than with a big juicy piece of prime rib? And when it's glazed with currants . . . why, we've gone over the top!

One 4- to 5-pound boneless beef rib eye roast
5 garlic cloves, minced
2 teaspoons dry mustard
1 teaspoon salt
1 teaspoon black pepper
1/3 cup currant jelly

Preheat the oven to 350°F. Line a roasting pan with aluminum foil and coat with nonstick cooking spray. Place the meat in the pan. In a small bowl, combine the garlic, mustard, salt, and pepper; mix well, then rub over the meat. Roast for 1 hour. Brush the currant jelly over the meat and roast for 20 to 30 minutes, or until a meat thermometer inserted in the center registers 150°F. for medium-rare, or until the desired doneness. Remove the meat to a cutting board and allow to sit for 10 to 15 minutes before carving across the grain.

GREAT GO-ALONG: This is heavenly served with a currant sauce. Here's how easy it is: Melt 1/2 cup currant jelly in a medium saucepan over medium-high heat. Stir in 1/2 cup Burgundy wine, 1 tablespoon cornstarch, and 1/4 teaspoon dry mustard. Bring to a boil and cook for 2 to 3 minutes, or until slightly thickened. That's it!

Yorkshire Pudding Popovers

6 popovers

Hmm, what should we serve with our tasty prime rib? How about some Yorkshire pudding? It *is* traditional to serve that on the side. Well, when you make it like this muffin-style version, there's no need to preheat any pans or worry about it rising, 'cause it's practically foolproof. And that's just what we need when we have lots to do! Oh—I recommend making extra, since these go down so easily!

2 eggs, chilled
1 cup cold milk
1 tablespoon butter, melted
1 cup all-purpose flour
2 scallions, thinly sliced
½ teaspoon garlic powder
½ teaspoon salt

Preheat the oven to 425°F. Coat a 6-cup muffin tin with nonstick cooking spray. In a large bowl, combine all the ingredients and beat with a wooden spoon until smooth. Immediately pour the batter into the muffin cups. Bake for 30 to 35 minutes, or until golden brown and puffy. Cool slightly before removing from the muffin cups. Serve immediately.

TIP: These will "pop" up better if you don't open the oven until nearly the end of the suggested cooking time. Then get ready to dunk them in the prime rib pan drippings or slather with plain or herbed butter. Yum!

90

Citrus-Honey Carrots

4 to 6 servings

Sometimes the simplest things are the best, like carrots glazed with honey. Why not make 'em and add a twist of lime zest for a nice touch of holiday green? Now that's the best, taken a step further.

2 tablespoons butter
¼ cup honey
2 cans (14½ ounces each) whole baby carrots, drained
1 teaspoon grated lime peel

Melt the butter in a large skillet over medium-high heat. Add the honey and cook for 1 to 2 minutes, or until the sauce has thickened, stirring frequently. Add the carrots and lime peel and sauté for 1 to 2 minutes, or until heated through and well coated with the sauce. Serve immediately.

TIP: For extra zest, grate a bit of additional lime peel over the top just before serving.

Christmas Goose

5 to 6 servings

There's a Christmas carol that goes like this: "Christmas is coming, the goose is getting fat . . ." Let's hope it's true, 'cause we want to serve the fattest, juiciest goose around. And when it's glazed with this citrus-sugar blend, it's sure to be extra-juicy and extra-crispy, too.

2 tangerines
¼ cup (½ stick) butter, melted, divided
½ teaspoon rubbed sage
½ teaspoon salt
¼ teaspoon black pepper
One 8- to 9-pound goose, thawed if frozen
2 tablespoons light brown sugar
1 cup orange juice
1 tablespoon cornstarch

TIP: If you pierce the skin before roasting your Christmas goose, it will be much less fatty and a lot more crispy.

Preheat the oven to 400°F. Finely grate the tangerine peel and set aside the tangerines. In a small bowl, combine the peel, half of the melted butter, the sage, salt, and pepper. Place the goose in a large roasting pan and rub the butter mixture evenly over the entire goose. Quarter the tangerines and place in the cavity of the goose. Roast for 30 minutes. Reduce the oven temperature to 325°F. and roast for 2¼ to 2½ hours longer, or until a meat thermometer registers 180°F. to 185°F., basting with the pan juices about every 30 minutes. Meanwhile, combine the remaining melted butter and the brown sugar in a small saucepan over medium-high heat; heat for 1 minute, or until the sugar is melted, stirring occasionally. In a small bowl, combine the orange juice and cornstarch; mix well and add to the butter mixture, stirring until thickened. Serve with the goose.

Cranberry-Orange Stuffing

6 to 9 servings

After you sit down and say grace, it'll be time for some serious eating. It's also time for stuffing. No, not the stockings, the side dish. This fruity version will be the hit of the meal!

    1 package (8 ounces) herb stuffing
    ½ cup sweetened dried cranberries
    1 rib celery, finely chopped
    1 can (11 ounces) mandarin oranges, drained
    1 can (14½ ounces) ready-to-use chicken broth
    6 tablespoons (¾ stick) butter, melted

Preheat the oven to 325°F. Coat an 8-inch square baking dish with nonstick cooking spray. In a large bowl, combine all the ingredients; mix well. Spoon into the baking dish and cover with aluminum foil. Bake for 20 minutes. Remove the aluminum foil and bake for 15 to 20 more minutes, or until heated through and golden.

Cheesy Mashed Potatoes

6 to 9 servings

To make the holiday season extra-special, it's important to surround yourself with all your favorite foods as well as your favorite people. That's why I knew I'd better include these savory mashed potatoes. They're a combination of everybody's favorites!

2¾ cups milk

3 tablespoons butter

2 cups instant mashed potato flakes

¾ teaspoon salt

½ teaspoon black pepper

½ small onion, finely chopped

1 garlic clove, minced

2 teaspoons freeze-dried chives

1 cup (4 ounces) shredded Swiss cheese, divided

1 egg, lightly beaten

Preheat the oven to 425°F. Coat an 8-inch square baking dish with nonstick cooking spray. In a medium saucepan, combine the milk and butter over medium heat until hot but not boiling, stirring occasionally. Remove from the heat and add the potato flakes, salt, and pepper; mix well. Add the onion, garlic, and chives; mix well. Add ¾ cup cheese and the egg; mix well. Spoon into the baking dish, then sprinkle the remaining ¼ cup cheese over the top. Bake for 25 to 30 minutes, or until golden. Serve immediately.

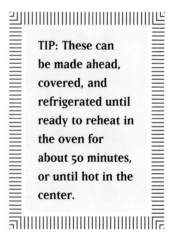

TIP: These can be made ahead, covered, and refrigerated until ready to reheat in the oven for about 50 minutes, or until hot in the center.

Steaming Green Bean Casserole

4 to 6 servings

Why is it that by the time all the food has passed around the table, the veggies are always cold? If you serve 'em like this, you'll have a piping-hot casserole that everybody will enjoy. (And it'll give you the perfect opportunity to use those Santa and Mrs. Claus potholders, too!)

1 can (10¾ ounces) condensed cream of chicken soup
1 tablespoon all-purpose flour
1 garlic clove, minced
1 package (16 ounces) frozen French cut green beans, thawed
1 package (16 ounces) frozen pearl onions, thawed and drained
1 jar (2 ounces) chopped pimientos, drained
½ cup crushed butter-flavored crackers
1 tablespoon butter, melted

LIGHTER TIP: Use reduced-fat soup and skip the butter and cracker topping. It'll still taste great!

Preheat the oven to 350°F. Coat an 8-inch square baking dish with nonstick cooking spray. In a medium bowl, combine the soup, flour, and garlic; mix well. Add the green beans, onions, and pimientos; mix well and spoon into the baking dish. In a small bowl, combine the crushed crackers and butter; mix well. Sprinkle over the top of the casserole and bake for 40 to 45 minutes, or until bubbly and the vegetables are tender.

Yule Log

10 to 12 servings

After those predinner nibbles and the big dinner, there's still a tiny bit of room left for dessert. Better use it for the traditional Bûche de Noël, otherwise known as a Yule log. Go ahead—chop off a piece and enjoy!

¾ cup all-purpose flour

1 teaspoon baking powder

¼ teaspoon salt

3 eggs

1 cup granulated sugar

⅓ cup water

2 teaspoons vanilla extract, divided

Grated peel of 1 orange

2 cups confectioners' sugar, plus more for sprinkling

⅓ cup unsweetened cocoa

¼ cup (½ stick) butter, softened

¼ cup milk

Preheat the oven to 375°F. Line a 10" × 15" rimmed baking sheet with aluminum foil and coat with nonstick cooking spray. In a small bowl, combine the flour, baking powder, and salt; mix well and set aside. In a large bowl, beat the eggs until frothy. Gradually beat in the granulated sugar, water, 1 teaspoon vanilla, and the orange peel until well blended. Gradually beat in the flour mixture just until smooth. Pour evenly into the baking sheet and bake for 10 to 12 minutes, or until a wooden toothpick inserted in the

center comes out clean. Sprinkle a clean kitchen towel with confectioners' sugar and invert the cake onto the towel; carefully peel off the aluminum foil. While hot, roll the cake and towel up jelly-roll style from a narrow end; cool on a wire rack. When cooled, unroll the cake, removing the towel. In a medium bowl, beat the confectioners' sugar, cocoa, butter, milk, and remaining 1 teaspoon vanilla until creamy. Reserve ½ cup of the frosting and spread the remainder over the cake. Roll the cake up again. Spread the reserved frosting over the outside of the cake. Lightly score the entire length of the log with the tines of a fork to look like bark. Chill for at least 2 hours before slicing and serving.

> **Did You Know . . .**
> the Yule log comes from a traditional European custom? On Christmas Eve, a giant freshly cut log was brought into the house to be blessed. Nowadays, most families favor a log made of cake and smothered in chocolate.

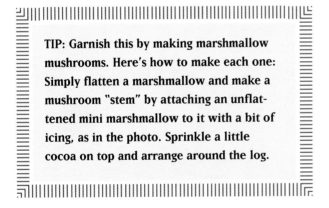

TIP: Garnish this by making marshmallow mushrooms. Here's how to make each one: Simply flatten a marshmallow and make a mushroom "stem" by attaching an unflattened mini marshmallow to it with a bit of icing, as in the photo. Sprinkle a little cocoa on top and arrange around the log.

White Chocolate Mousse Cake

16 servings

Animals have always played an important part in Christmas celebrations. There are donkeys and camels in the manger scene and Santa's sleigh is led by reindeer. And now there's one more added to the Christmas lineup: a moose. Actually, it's an M-O-U-S-S-E—a white chocolate one . . . it's gotta be the best-tasting kind!

1 package (12 ounces) vanilla wafer cookies,
    finely crushed

½ cup (1 stick) butter, melted

2 eggs

4 egg yolks

2 packages (11 ounces each) white chocolate chips

2 cups (1 pint) heavy cream

⅓ cup confectioners' sugar

1 jar (10 ounces) red maraschino cherries,
    drained and quartered

1 jar (6 ounces) green maraschino cherries,
    drained and quartered

16 stemmed red maraschino cherries,
    well drained

In a medium bowl, combine the crushed vanilla wafers and butter; mix well. Press over the bottom and sides of a 10-inch springform pan to form a crust; chill. In a small bowl, combine the eggs and egg yolks; mix well and set aside. Melt the white chocolate chips in a large saucepan over low heat for 3 to 4 minutes, stirring constantly. Add the egg mixture and quickly whisk until well blended; cook for about 5 minutes, until thick and glossy, stirring occasionally. Remove from the heat and set aside to cool to room temperature. Meanwhile, in a medium bowl, beat the heavy cream until soft peaks form. Add the confectioners' sugar and beat until stiff peaks form. Fold into the white chocolate mixture until well blended. Stir in the chopped red and green cherries and spoon into the prepared crust. Place the stemmed cherries around the edge of the cake. Cover and freeze for at least 8 hours, or until firm.

Christmas Morning

🎄 This symbol indicates my "make-aheads" that can be prepared in advance.

It's Christmas morning and when you take a look around the family room, all you can see is scattered wrapping paper and ribbons, presents and empty boxes, and, yes, a bunch of hungry people ready for a satisfying Christmas breakfast. After all, opening presents is hard work, so I've got a bunch of ways to help you get ready to feed the troops and keep them in the Christmas spirit.

Since most families eat a big meal later in the day, why not serve a breakfast or brunch buffet—muffins, maybe a fruit salad, and an egg dish along with coffees, teas, and different hot cocoa flavors for the kids. It's quick and easy—just what we need right about now.

In fact, many of the dishes in this chapter are marked with a 🐿. These are my "make-aheads" that can be prepared in advance. Be sure to read the tips that accompany these recipes for any special instructions.

You know, keeping the Christmas morning meal simple means you'll spend less time in the kitchen and more time with the family. That's the best gift of all!

Rise-and-Shine Ham Frittata

4 to 6 servings

Here's the deal. First you dig into the Christmas stockings, then you jump into the kitchen and put together the ingredients for this frittata. Into the oven it goes (don't forget to set the timer). Then back to those Christmas gifts you go. By the time you hear the buzzer, the unwrapping will be "wrapping up" and everybody will be ready for some serious eating.

1 dozen eggs
½ cup milk
1 pound deli ham, diced
½ cup (2 ounces) shredded mozzarella cheese
3 scallions, thinly sliced
1 small red bell pepper, finely chopped

TIP: You can mix all these ingredients together the night before, pour into the baking dish, cover, and chill until morning. Then all you'll need to do on Christmas morning is bake the frittata.

Preheat the oven to 400°F. Coat an 8-inch square baking dish with nonstick cooking spray. In a medium bowl, whisk the eggs and milk until well combined. Add the remaining ingredients; mix well. Pour into the baking dish and bake for 45 to 55 minutes, or until firm in the center. Allow to sit for 5 minutes, then cut and serve.

Did You Know . . .
there's an easy way to tell if an egg is fresh? Fill a bowl with water and lower the egg into it. If the egg sinks, it's a keeper. If it floats, get rid of it . . . fast!

This symbol indicates my "make-aheads" that can be prepared in advance.

Holiday Sausage Roll-ups

16 rolls

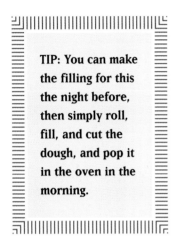

TIP: You can make the filling for this the night before, then simply roll, fill, and cut the dough, and pop it in the oven in the morning.

Sure, it's easy to toss doughnuts and bagels onto the table, but the gang is probably looking for something a little fancier on this special day. Here you go—a holiday sausage roll-up in the shape of a Christmas tree.

1 package (16 ounces) spicy pork sausage (such as Jimmy Dean)
½ medium red bell pepper, diced
4 scallions, thinly sliced
2 packages (8 ounces each) refrigerated crescent rolls (8 rolls each)

Preheat the oven to 400°F. In a medium bowl, combine the sausage, red pepper, and scallions; mix well. Unroll one package of crescent rolls and press the seams together to form one large rectangle. Repeat with the second package of crescent rolls. Spread half of the sausage mixture evenly over each rectangle; starting from a narrow end, roll up jelly-roll style. Cut each roll into eight equal slices and place on their sides on a baking sheet to form a Christmas tree (see photo). Bake for 25 to 30 minutes, or until the sausage is no longer pink and the crust is golden. Serve warm.

🌿 Apple Strudel

6 to 8 servings

The coffee's brewed, the sausage roll-ups are in the oven, and the eggs are ready to go. It's time to make the home-made apple strudel. Yes, homemade. But don't worry, it's very easy. Just consider this recipe one of my Christmas gifts to you.

    1 sheet frozen puff pastry (from a 17.25-ounce package),
        thawed
    ⅓ cup sugar
    2 teaspoons ground cinnamon
    1 can (20 ounces) sliced apples, drained
    ⅓ cup raisins
    1 egg, beaten

Preheat the oven to 400°F. Place the pastry on a cookie sheet and unfold. In a medium bowl, combine the sugar and cinnamon; mix well. Reserve 2 teaspoons of the sugar mixture. Add the apples and raisins to the remaining mixture; mix well. Let sit for about 2 minutes; drain off any excess liquid. Spoon the mixture down the center of the dough. Cut slits in the dough 1 inch apart lengthwise down each side of the filling. Brush each 1-inch dough strip with the beaten egg and fold over the dough as shown. Brush the top of the pastry with the remaining egg and sprinkle with the reserved sugar mixture. Bake for 20 to 25 minutes, or until golden. Serve warm, or allow to cool before serving.

🌿 This symbol indicates my "make-aheads" that can be prepared in advance.

From the Kitchen Of:

SANTA

Recipe: **APPLE STRUDEL**

1 sheet puff pastry dough
1/3 cup sugar
2 teaspoons ground cinnamon
1 can sliced apples, drained

❦ Jolly French Toast

8 servings

Christmas Eve is usually pretty busy for everyone, especially parents of young ones. After the plate of cookies and glass of milk are set out for Santa and the kiddies hit the hay, the real work begins. Presents must be wrapped and put under the tree, stockings need to be filled, and the cookies and milk have to be tended to (you know what I mean!). If you can take an extra minute to whip up this baked French toast, then, come morning, the oven will be working alone!

> 1 loaf (12 ounces) French bread, cut into 8 slices
> 6 eggs
> 2 cups (1 pint) half-and-half
> ½ cup sugar
> ½ teaspoon ground cinnamon
> ½ teaspoon ground nutmeg
> ½ teaspoon salt

Coat a 9" × 13" baking dish with nonstick cooking spray. Place the bread slices in a single layer in the baking dish. In a medium bowl, combine the remaining ingredients; mix well and pour over the bread slices. Cover and chill for at least 30 minutes, or until the liquid has been absorbed. Preheat the oven to 400°F. Bake for 35 to 40 minutes, or until golden brown.

GREAT GO-ALONG: Try this simple maple vanilla syrup: In a medium saucepan, combine 1 cup maple syrup, ½ cup (1 stick) butter, and 1 teaspoon vanilla extract over low heat and cook for 2 to 3 minutes, or until the butter is melted and the mixture is well combined, stirring frequently. Serve warm over the French toast.

❦ This symbol indicates my "make-aheads" that can be prepared in advance. Reheat this just before serving.

Fruit Foster

6 to 8 servings

If you've ever visited New Orleans, you've most likely tried bananas Foster. If you haven't been there or tried this specialty, just imagine this: a bubbling combination of sliced bananas cooked with butter, brown sugar, and rum. Mmm, mmm! Now, that may be a little too much work for first thing Christmas morning, but this version isn't . . . and it's just as tasty as the original. (See photo page 107.)

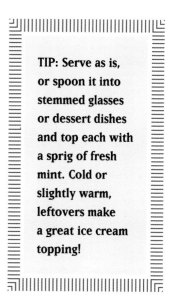

TIP: Serve as is, or spoon it into stemmed glasses or dessert dishes and top each with a sprig of fresh mint. Cold or slightly warm, leftovers make a great ice cream topping!

¾ cup firmly packed light brown sugar
½ cup (1 stick) butter
1 can (29 ounces) pear halves, drained
1 can (29 ounces) peach halves, drained
1 can (20 ounces) pineapple slices, drained
1 can (11 ounces) mandarin oranges, drained
1 jar (6 ounces) maraschino cherries, drained

Preheat the oven to 325°F. In a medium saucepan, combine the brown sugar and butter over medium heat until the butter melts and the sugar dissolves, stirring constantly; remove from the heat. In a 9" × 13" baking dish, combine the remaining ingredients; mix well. Pour the brown sugar mixture over the fruit and bake for 55 to 60 minutes, or until hot and bubbly. Serve immediately.

This symbol indicates my "make-aheads" that can be prepared in advance. Reheat this just before serving.

Cranberry-Walnut Muffins

1 dozen muffins

Muffins are an old favorite served at almost any special breakfast or brunch. There's nothing tastier than a warm, moist muffin slathered with a favorite spread. Why not make something a bit above the ordinary? When you serve these festive muffins right out of the oven on Christmas morning, everybody'll know it's gonna be a very merry day.

1¼ cups plus 2 tablespoons firmly packed light brown sugar, divided
¼ cup chopped walnuts
3 cups all-purpose flour
4 teaspoons baking powder
¾ teaspoon salt
1⅓ cups milk
2 eggs
½ cup (1 stick) butter, softened
1½ cups fresh cranberries, chopped
Grated peel of 1 orange

TIP: This makes large muffins, so, depending on the type of muffin tin you use, the muffin tops may run together. If they do, just use a table knife to cut between the muffins before removing them from the tin.

Preheat the oven to 400°F. Coat a 12-cup muffin tin with nonstick cooking spray. In a small bowl, combine 2 tablespoons brown sugar and the walnuts; mix well and set aside. In a large bowl, combine the flour, the remaining 1¼ cups brown sugar, the baking powder, and salt; mix well. In another small bowl, whisk the milk and eggs until well blended. Add to the flour mixture, along with the butter; beat until just combined. Fold in the cranberries and orange peel. Pour into the muffin cups and sprinkle with the reserved walnut mixture. Bake for 20 to 25 minutes, or until a wooden toothpick inserted in the center comes out clean. Allow to cool slightly, then remove to a wire rack to cool completely.

Peanut-Butter-Cup Cocoa

about 2 quarts, 6 to 8 servings

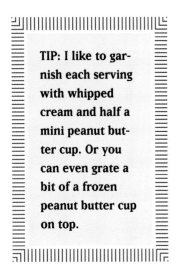

TIP: I like to garnish each serving with whipped cream and half a mini peanut butter cup. Or you can even grate a bit of a frozen peanut butter cup on top.

What's missing in this picture: a tall Christmas tree shining bright, a roaring fire in the fireplace, and the gang listening to carols on the stereo? Big steaming mugs of hot cocoa—that's what. It's so easy! And instead of plain old cocoa, be adventurous and try this new variation.

4 cups (1 quart) milk
4 cups (2 pints) half-and-half
1½ cups sugar
1 cup unsweetened cocoa
1 cup creamy peanut butter
2 tablespoons vanilla extract

In a soup pot, combine the milk, half-and-half, sugar, and cocoa over medium heat and cook until the mixture just begins to boil, stirring constantly. Remove from the heat and add the peanut butter and vanilla. Whisk until smooth and creamy. Serve immediately.

Flavored Whipped Cream Dollops

about 12 dollops

Christmas morning isn't just any old morning, so why serve the same old coffee? It's nice to jazz it up with flavored whipped cream dollops. How about topping yours with a vanilla dollop, or almond, or the cool taste of peppermint? Know the best part? We can keep these in the freezer for everyday, not just special occasions.

1 cup (½ pint) heavy cream
3 tablespoons confectioners' sugar

VANILLA WHIPPED CREAM DOLLOPS

1 tablespoon vanilla extract

ALMOND WHIPPED CREAM DOLLOPS

1 tablespoon almond extract

PEPPERMINT WHIPPED CREAM DOLLOPS

2 teaspoons peppermint extract

Line a baking sheet with waxed paper. In a medium bowl, beat the cream and sugar until stiff peaks form. Add the desired flavored extract to the whipped cream; mix well. Spoon heaping tablespoon-sized dollops onto the baking sheet and freeze for about 1½ hours, or until firm. Remove from the baking sheet and store in an airtight container or resealable plastic storage bag in the freezer until ready to use.

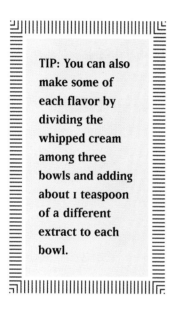

TIP: You can also make some of each flavor by dividing the whipped cream among three bowls and adding about 1 teaspoon of a different extract to each bowl.

This symbol indicates my "make-aheads" that can be prepared in advance.

Christmas Dinner

By now all the gifts have either been tried on or played with, and we've said our thank-yous. The Christmas parades on TV are over and the turkey's roasting in the oven. As the scent makes its way through the house, tummies are bound to start grumbling. That means it's almost time for Christmas dinner. And what a dinner you can have in store for everybody! This year why not go all out and surprise the gang? Instead of the same thing you always serve, try a few new twists like angel biscuits, apple-glazed turkey, and hearty sausage stuffing. You won't believe how easy it can be! Why, it'll seem like another Christmas gift!

Angel Biscuits

about 1 dozen biscuits

Why not invite an angel or two to Christmas dinner? Let me tell you, they'll certainly be welcomed!

2¼ cups biscuit baking mix
⅔ cup milk
3 tablespoons butter, melted
3 tablespoons grated Parmesan cheese

Preheat the oven to 425°F. In a large bowl, combine the biscuit baking mix and milk, stirring until a dough forms. Lightly flour a work surface and knead the dough until smooth. With a lightly floured rolling pin, roll out the dough to a ¼-inch thickness. Using an angel-shaped cookie cutter, cut out the dough and place 1 inch apart on ungreased baking sheets. In a small bowl, combine the butter and Parmesan cheese; mix well and brush over the angel shapes. Bake for 8 to 10 minutes, or until light golden. Serve immediately, or remove to a wire rack to cool completely.

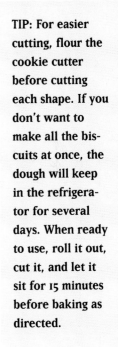

TIP: For easier cutting, flour the cookie cutter before cutting each shape. If you don't want to make all the biscuits at once, the dough will keep in the refrigerator for several days. When ready to use, roll it out, cut it, and let it sit for 15 minutes before baking as directed.

Salad Wreath

6 to 8 servings

Toss away the idea of a plain tossed salad with the used Christmas wrapping paper. This year, try something new that's easy to prepare and a whole lot more exciting.

2 packages (4 ounces each) mixed baby greens
12 small cherry tomatoes
4 slices American cheese
1 medium cucumber, cut into ¼-inch slices
1 large carrot

Place a small bowl in the center of a large round platter and fill with your favorite dressing (see Great Go-Along). Form a wreath as in the photograph, as follows: Arrange the baby greens around the small bowl. Place the tomatoes in clusters of three on the greens. Using Christmas cookie cutters, cut each slice of cheese into a holiday shape and place over the greens. Arrange the cucumber slices around the edge of the platter. Using a vegetable peeler, peel wide thick strips from the carrot. Loop the strips to create a bow. Serve, or cover and chill until ready to serve.

Did You Know . . .
there's actually a temporary employment service for Santas? Western Staff Services trains over three thousand "helper" Santas to appear at malls, department stores, and hospitals.

Apple-Glazed Turkey

8 to 10 servings

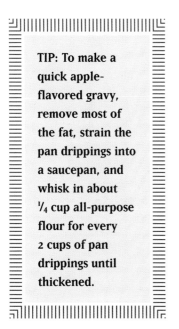

TIP: To make a quick apple-flavored gravy, remove most of the fat, strain the pan drippings into a saucepan, and whisk in about ¼ cup all-purpose flour for every 2 cups of pan drippings until thickened.

I got this idea from a viewer who wrote and shared her successful orange-glazed turkey recipe. She told me that every Christmas her turkey platter is practically licked clean! She never has any leftovers. This got me thinking about other flavors that we could use as a glaze, so one day I tried apples and the turkey came out juicier than ever. I suggest cooking a larger bird than normal, so there'll be some juicy leftovers.

One 12- to 14-pound turkey
1 teaspoon salt
½ teaspoon black pepper
3 apples, cored and quartered
1 container (12 ounces) frozen apple juice
    concentrate, thawed
1 can (14½ ounces) ready-to-use chicken broth
1½ teaspoons rubbed sage

Preheat the oven to 325°F. Line a roasting pan with aluminum foil and place the turkey in it. Rub the turkey inside and out with the salt and pepper; place the apples inside the cavity. Pour the apple juice concentrate evenly over the turkey. Pour the chicken broth into the pan. Sprinkle the sage evenly over the top of the turkey. Cover loosely with aluminum foil and roast for 3 hours, basting with the pan juices every 30 minutes. Remove the foil and roast for 30 to 60 more minutes, or until no pink remains and the juices run clear. Allow to sit for 15 minutes before carving.

Cranberry Relish Squares

16 squares

Sure, we can simply open a can of cranberry sauce and set that on the table, but why should we when this recipe doesn't take much more work than opening that can, and it's so much tastier.

1 can (11 ounces) mandarin oranges, drained
3 packages (4-serving size) cranberry-flavored gelatin
2 cups boiling water
1 can (16 ounces) whole-berry cranberry sauce
1 cup chopped pecans

Reserve 16 orange sections for garnish; chop the remaining orange sections. Place the gelatin in a medium bowl and add the boiling water; stir to dissolve the gelatin. Add the cranberry sauce, pecans, and chopped oranges; mix well. Pour into an 8-inch square baking dish; cover and chill for at least 4 hours, or until set. Cut into squares and garnish with the reserved orange sections.

TIP: These can be made several days in advance, covered, and stored in the refrigerator until needed. If you can't find cranberry-flavored gelatin, any red one, like strawberry or cherry, will work.

Sausage Stuffing

6 to 8 servings

You know me—I believe you can use any brands and adapt recipes to your gang's favorite tastes. And that's what this recipe is all about. We start with prepared stuffing and fancy it up with a few off-the-shelf ingredients. Yes, it's okay to use a shortcut or two, even on Christmas.

1 medium onion, chopped
½ cup (1 stick) butter, melted, divided
1 package (16 ounces) ground pork sausage
¼ pound fresh mushrooms, chopped
1 can (14½ ounces) reduced-sodium ready-to-use chicken broth
1 package (8 ounces) corn bread stuffing
½ cup chopped almonds, toasted (optional)
1 egg, beaten

Preheat the oven to 325°F. In a large skillet, sauté the onion in 1 tablespoon butter over medium-high heat for 5 to 7 minutes, or until golden. Add the sausage and mushrooms and sauté for 3 to 5 minutes, or until the sausage is browned and the mushrooms are tender; drain, if necessary, and set aside. In a large bowl, combine the chicken broth, stuffing, and the almonds, if desired; mix well. Add the remaining 7 tablespoons melted butter, the sausage mixture, and the egg; mix well. Spoon into an 8-inch square baking dish or a mold. Cover with aluminum foil and bake for 30 minutes. Uncover and bake for 30 to 35 more minutes, or until heated through and the top is golden.

TIP: You can bake this in almost any type of oven-proof Christmas shaped mold. It's nice to use a Christmas tree mold and decorate the "tree" with cooked peas and carrots.

LIGHTER TIP: It's easy to lighten up almost any stuffing by substituting chicken stock for half or more of the melted butter. And you can usually use chopped celery in place of nuts.

Sweet Potato Surprise

6 to 8 servings

Everyone loves surprises around Christmastime, but why limit those surprises to gifts? Bring them into holiday meals, too! Now, if you can keep a secret, I'll tell you: The surprise here is a combination of mandarin oranges and toasted coconut marshmallows . . . and it makes for the sweetest-tasting dinner surprise I know!

2 cans (29 ounces each) sweet potatoes or yams, drained
3 eggs
¼ cup sugar
½ teaspoon ground cinnamon
¼ teaspoon ground nutmeg
1 can (11 ounces) mandarin oranges, drained
1 package (10 ounces) toasted coconut marshmallows
    (see Tip)

Preheat the oven to 350°F. Coat an 8-inch square baking dish with nonstick cooking spray. In a large bowl, mash the sweet potatoes, then add the eggs, sugar, cinnamon, and nutmeg; mix well. Stir in the mandarin oranges until well combined. Spoon half of the sweet potato mixture into the baking dish and top with half of the marshmallows. Top with the remaining sweet potato mixture and bake for 50 minutes. Top with the remaining marshmallows and bake for 5 to 7 minutes, or until heated through and the marshmallows have melted.

TIP: Toasted coconut marshmallows are simply regular-sized marshmallows that are covered with toasted coconut. They should be available in the supermarket near the plain marshmallows. If you can't find them, regular marshmallows will work, too.

Very Merry Vegetable Medley

4 to 6 servings

Since the dinner table's going to look a little different this year with all your new main dishes, why not try out a few different side dishes, too? For instance, instead of serving the old ho-hum mushy vegetables, you can whip up this colorful sautéed veggie medley. Your gang will applaud you for being so creative.

3 tablespoons butter
3 medium bell peppers (1 each red, green, and yellow),
   cut into thin strips
1 medium onion, thinly sliced
1 garlic clove, minced
1 large zucchini, cut into thin strips
½ teaspoon salt
¼ teaspoon black pepper

Melt the butter in a medium skillet over medium-high heat. Add the bell peppers, onion, and garlic and sauté for 4 to 5 minutes, or until crisp-tender. Add the remaining ingredients and sauté for 2 to 3 minutes, or until the vegetables are tender. Serve immediately.

Creamy Peppermint Cheesecake

6 to 8 servings

A friend of mine was invited to her aunt's for Christmas dinner and was asked to bring a dessert. Her aunt had asked four other people to bring desserts, too. And guess what? They all brought pecan pie! After I heard that, I gave her this recipe, 'cause it's quick, easy, and rarely duplicated.

2 packages (8 ounces each) cream cheese, softened
½ cup sugar
2 eggs
¾ cup sour cream
1 teaspoon vanilla extract
1 teaspoon peppermint extract
6 drops red food coloring
One 9-inch graham cracker pie crust
Whipped cream and candy canes for garnish (optional)

Preheat the oven to 350°F. In a large bowl, beat the cream cheese and sugar until light and fluffy. Add the eggs and beat well. Add the sour cream and vanilla; mix well. Place ½ cup of the mixture in a small bowl and stir in the peppermint extract and food coloring; mix well. Pour the remaining cream cheese mixture into the pie crust. Smooth the top. Drop the peppermint mixture by spoonfuls into the mixture in the crust and swirl with a knife to create a marbled effect. Bake for 30 to 35 minutes, or until the edges are set (the center will be slightly loose). Allow to cool for 1 hour, then cover and chill for at least 6 hours before serving. To serve, top each slice with a dollop of whipped cream and a miniature candy cane, if desired.

TIP: If you can sneak an extra few moments, make your own home-made graham cracker crust.

Caramel Bread Pudding

6 to 8 servings

Boy, I love bread pudding. Serve it hot and I'm happy. Serve it cold and I'm happy, too. Now imagine bread pudding laced with warm, gooey caramel! All we need to add is some fresh whipped cream and Christmas dinner will be complete.

1 loaf (1 pound) day-old French or Italian bread, torn into
    1-inch pieces
2 cups warm water
3 eggs
1 cup (½ pint) heavy cream
30 caramels, chopped
½ cup granulated sugar
1 teaspoon vanilla extract
1 teaspoon salt

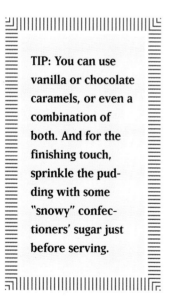

TIP: You can use vanilla or chocolate caramels, or even a combination of both. And for the finishing touch, sprinkle the pudding with some "snowy" confectioners' sugar just before serving.

Preheat the oven to 350°F. Coat an 8-inch square baking dish with nonstick cooking spray. In a large bowl, toss together the bread and water, soaking the bread. In a small bowl, whisk the eggs; stir in the heavy cream. Add to the soaked bread, along with the remaining ingredients; mix well. Place in the baking dish and bake for 60 to 65 minutes, or until the center is firm. Serve warm, or allow to cool completely, cover, and chill.

Country Christmas

When I think of country-style cooking, I think of the tastes of homemade jams, pickles, and relishes, and the smells of fresh-baked breads and pies. Mmm, mmm!

It's those tastes and smells that create the comfort and warmth found in country homes all throughout the year, but especially at holiday times.

And here's our opportunity to create some new traditions with our very own country Christmas. Whether you've done this before or it's the first time, I hope the following recipes will add just the right touch of country flavor and charm to this year's holiday celebration.

Piping-Hot Corn Bread

Piping-Hot Corn Bread

10 to 12 slices

Homemade breads are a staple in most country kitchens and, whatever the meal, they're almost always served piping hot from the oven. Trust me—there's nothing like a hot slab of fresh bread slathered with creamy butter. Unfortunately, with all our other Christmas chores, it's hard to find the time to bake fresh bread. Well, here's a fast and easy version of country corn bread that'll do you proud in *any* season. Oh, don't forget the butter!

3 tablespoons butter
1 small onion, finely chopped
1 package (8½ ounces) corn muffin mix
1 container (3 ounces) real bacon bits
3 eggs
½ cup chicken broth
½ teaspoon hot pepper sauce
2 teaspoons rubbed sage

Preheat the oven to 350°F. Coat a 9" × 5" loaf pan with nonstick cooking spray. Melt the butter in a medium skillet over medium-high heat. Add the onion and sauté for 3 to 5 minutes, or until tender. Place in a large bowl and add the remaining ingredients; mix well. Spoon into the loaf pan and bake for 25 to 30 minutes, or until a wooden toothpick inserted in the center comes out clean. Allow to cool for 5 minutes, then remove from the pan and slice. Serve warm.

TIP: You can make this in mini loaf pans or muffin tins, too. Just reduce the baking time accordingly.

GREAT GO-ALONG: Treat your family extra-special by serving this with honey butter that you made from scratch by combining ½ cup (1 stick) softened butter with 2 tablespoons honey until smooth and creamy.

Pumpkin Cheesecake Soup

8 to 10 servings

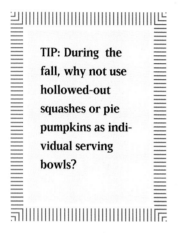

TIP: During the fall, why not use hollowed-out squashes or pie pumpkins as individual serving bowls?

When we've got overflowing harvest-time gardens, we can get creative with our autumn dishes. I know all about this from my childhood, 'cause my father was always bringing home bushels of peppers or tomatoes for my mom to use however she could. Well, that's how pumpkin soup was first made—by using the bounty of the harvest. Unfortunately, pumpkins aren't available year-round, so at other times of the year we used canned—and we happily found out they were more convenient than fresh.

2 cans (30 ounces each) pumpkin pie mix
2 cans (14½ ounces each) ready-to-use chicken broth
2 cups (1 pint) half-and-half
1 cup sour cream
Nutmeg for garnish, optional

In a soup pot, whisk the pumpkin pie mix and chicken broth over medium-high heat and cook for 7 to 8 minutes, until hot. Slowly stir in the half-and-half and cook for 2 to 3 minutes, until heated through. Top each serving with a dollop of sour cream and a sprinkle of nutmeg, if desired.

Pineapple-Crusted Ham

6 to 8 servings

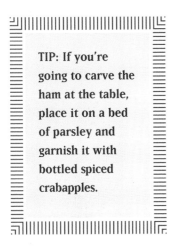

TIP: If you're going to carve the ham at the table, place it on a bed of parsley and garnish it with bottled spiced crabapples.

There's nothing like a country-style cured ham. One of my viewers shared her mother's way of preparing her traditional Christmas ham. First she would soak the ham for at least two days to get most of the salt out. Then she would let it simmer on the stovetop for an entire day. By the time it made its way to their table, the ham was so juicy it was practically falling off the bone. Sure, that's great if you have three whole days to make one ham, but most of us want it done quicker. Ta da! Here's a shortcut version, perfect for that special country Christmas dinner. And yes, it's still juicy as can be.

1 can (20 ounces) crushed pineapple, drained
1 cup firmly packed light brown sugar
1 cup applesauce
¼ cup cornstarch
¼ teaspoon ground cloves
One 5- to 6-pound fully cooked semi-boneless cured ham

Did You Know . . . to save roasting time, you can buy ham already cooked? Just read the labels and buy one that says "fully cooked." Then all you have to do is reheat and serve!

Preheat the oven to 375°F. Line a roasting pan with aluminum foil, then coat with nonstick cooking spray. In a medium bowl, combine all the ingredients except the ham; mix well. Place the ham in the roasting pan. Pat the pineapple mixture over the ham, coating completely. Bake for 1½ to 1¾ hours, or until heated through and the coating is crisp and brown, spooning the pineapple mixture over the ham every 20 minutes. Slice and serve.

Country Corn Relish

6 to 8 servings

One of those special touches I like to add to holiday foods is to give them more color. This corn relish is the perfect example, 'cause it's loaded with so many bright colors, especially the red and green of Christmas. Maybe that's why it's traditional for so many people to serve this relish at holiday time. You know me—I never like to mess with tradition!

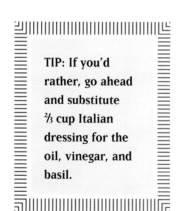

TIP: If you'd rather, go ahead and substitute ⅔ cup Italian dressing for the oil, vinegar, and basil.

⅓ cup vegetable oil
¼ cup cider vinegar
¼ cup chopped fresh parsley
2 teaspoons sugar
½ teaspoon dried basil
¼ teaspoon crushed red pepper
2 cans (15¼ ounces each) whole-kernel corn, drained
3 scallions, thinly sliced
2 large tomatoes, diced
1 medium green bell pepper, diced

In a large bowl, combine the oil, vinegar, parsley, sugar, basil, and crushed red pepper; mix well. Add the remaining ingredients and stir until well combined. Cover and chill for several hours, or overnight, before serving.

Home-Style Green Beans

8 to 10 servings

When we think of country cooking, we definitely think of it including lots of farm-fresh produce. This recipe came from a viewer who told me she likes to sauté Italian green beans from her husband's garden with tomatoes that she dries after the fall harvest. This combination is very trendy today yet country-delicious. To make it really easy, I substituted frozen Italian beans and a jar of sun-dried tomatoes.

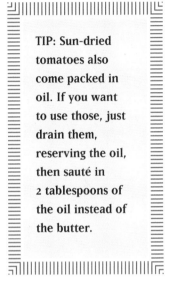

TIP: Sun-dried tomatoes also come packed in oil. If you want to use those, just drain them, reserving the oil, then sauté in 2 tablespoons of the oil instead of the butter.

2 tablespoons butter
½ cup dry-packed sun-dried tomatoes, reconstituted and slivered (see Tip)
⅓ cup chopped walnuts
2 garlic cloves, minced
3 packages (9 ounces each) frozen Italian green beans, thawed
¾ teaspoon salt

Melt the butter in a medium skillet over medium-high heat. Add the sun-dried tomatoes, walnuts, and garlic and sauté for 1 minute. Add the green beans and salt and sauté for 6 to 7 minutes, or until the beans are tender. Serve immediately.

Patchwork Potatoes

9 to 12 servings

Patchwork quilts have become a luxury, and they're certainly a big part of country decorating. Take a peek in a cozy bedroom and you're almost sure to see one hanging on the wall or draped over a bed piled with goose-feather pillows. In fact, quilting circles are popular again, with people getting together to socialize and work on quilts together. And the finished ones truly are pieces of artwork. At holiday time, why not think about creating a patchwork piece of art—for the table, not the bed. Yup, these patchwork potatoes will warm our tummies from the *inside* out.

> 4 cups warm mashed potatoes
> ¼ cup (½ stick) butter, melted, divided
> 1 teaspoon chopped fresh dill
> ¼ teaspoon black pepper
> 2 cans (29 ounces each) yams or sweet potatoes, drained
> Grated peel of 1 lemon

Preheat the oven to 350°F. Coat an 8-inch square baking dish with nonstick cooking spray. In a medium bowl, combine the mashed potatoes, 2 tablespoons melted butter, the dill, and pepper; mix well and set aside. In another medium bowl, mash the yams, then add the lemon peel and the remaining 2 tablespoons melted butter; mix well. Spoon five equal-sized scoops of the yam mixture into the baking dish, placing one scoop in each corner and one scoop in the center. Using a spoon, shape each scoop into a square. Place the mashed potato mixture in the four empty squares, dividing it equally. Pat down evenly to fill any gaps, forming a checkerboard pattern. Bake for 45 to 50 minutes, or until heated through.

Old-fashioned Steamed Pudding

12 to 16 servings

Some people may shy away from anything with mince-meat in it, 'cause they think that it's really minced meat. Actually, today's mincemeat is a combination of a few spices, nuts, and chopped fruits like raisins and apples. Add a few more ingredients to prepared mincemeat while slowly steaming it and we get a flavorful old-fashioned classic. Simply top it with some rum sauce (see Great Go-Along), and I guarantee there'll be no mincing words here—this pudding is tops!

> 1 cup (2 sticks) butter, softened
> 1 cup sugar
> 1 cup milk
> 4 eggs
> 1 container (20½ ounces) mincemeat with rum and brandy
> 2 cups pecans, chopped
> 1 cup all-purpose flour
> 7 slices white bread, torn into small pieces

Coat a 10-inch Bundt pan or tube pan with nonstick cooking spray. In a large bowl, beat the butter, sugar, milk, and eggs until well combined. Add the remaining ingredients and beat until well combined. Pour into the prepared

pan and cover tightly with aluminum foil. Fill a large soup pot halfway with hot water and place the pan in the pot. Cover and cook over medium heat for 2½ hours. Remove the pan from the pot and allow to cool for 15 minutes. Uncover and invert the pudding onto a serving platter. Serve warm, or allow to cool before serving.

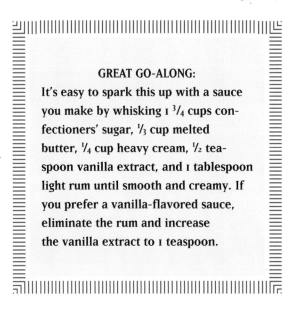

GREAT GO-ALONG:
It's easy to spark this up with a sauce you make by whisking 1 ³/₄ cups confectioners' sugar, ¹/₃ cup melted butter, ¹/₄ cup heavy cream, ¹/₂ teaspoon vanilla extract, and 1 tablespoon light rum until smooth and creamy. If you prefer a vanilla-flavored sauce, eliminate the rum and increase the vanilla extract to 1 teaspoon.

Pistachio Poinsettia Cake

12 to 16 servings

It doesn't matter if we're walking through the mall or down the street, at this time of year we're bound to see lots and lots of bright red poinsettias. They sure say, "Merry Christmas!" Don't they? So when it comes to our desserts, wouldn't it be nice to serve one that's just as inviting during the holidays? Here it is!

1 package (18.25 ounces) white cake mix
3 packages (4-serving size) instant pistachio pudding and
   pie filling
1½ cups milk, divided
½ cup vegetable oil
½ cup water
5 eggs
1 cup (½ pint) heavy cream
1 cup sweetened flaked coconut
¼ cup sugar
4 large red gumdrops
1 large green gumdrop

Preheat the oven to 350°F. Coat two 9-inch round cake pans with nonstick cooking spray, then dust with flour. In a large bowl, beat the cake mix, 2 packages pudding mix, ½ cup milk, the oil, and water until smooth. Beat in the

eggs until well combined. Divide equally between the cake pans and bake for 30 to 35 minutes, or until a wooden toothpick inserted in the center comes out clean. Allow to cool for 15 minutes, then remove to a wire rack to cool completely. In a medium bowl, beat the heavy cream and the remaining 1 cup milk and package of pudding mix until thickened. Frost the cake. Sprinkle the coconut evenly over the top and sides. Sprinkle a cutting board with the sugar, then place the gumdrops on top. Using a rolling pin, roll out each gumdrop to a 3-inch circle, pressing the flattened gumdrops into the sugar as they become sticky. Using a knife, cut poinsettia leaves out of the red and green gumdrops. Form a poinsettia in the center of the cake. Cover loosely and chill for at least 2 hours before serving.

> **Did You Know . . .**
> poinsettia plants, the ones traditionally associated with Christmas, grow in red, white, and pink varieties?

Cranberry Wassail

12 to 16 servings

TIP: I like to garnish this with apple and orange slices. To make sure the wassail stays warm, put it out in a slow cooker and let everyone help themselves to this delicious drink.

Some people think that "wassail" is just a toast, meaning "Good health to you!" That's not the case. It's also a drink. And, as the tradition goes, carolers would come to a house and exchange a few songs for a cup of this warm fruity punch. So, "Fa-la-la-la-la la-la-la-la" to you from me! (Now can I have a sip?)

1 container (64 ounces) apple cider
3 cups water
2 cups orange juice
1 container (12 ounces) frozen cranberry-raspberry juice concentrate
4 cinnamon sticks
6 whole cloves

In a soup pot, bring all the ingredients to a boil over high heat. Reduce the heat to low and simmer for 15 minutes. Serve warm.

Poached Candy Apples

4 servings

When you put these apples on your menu, you'd better put out the welcome mat and get ready for some old-fashioned good taste, too. Garnish them with a few sprigs of fresh mint and they'll look so pretty you won't want to eat 'em, but please do—or you'll miss out on a load of sweet-and-spicy down-home flavor!

1 cup red-hot cinnamon candies
3 cups apple cider
4 large apples, peeled
Fresh mint leaves, optional

In a large saucepan over medium heat, melt the cinnamon candies in the apple cider. Add the apples and spoon the sauce over the tops to coat. Reduce the heat to low, cover, and cook for 20 to 25 minutes, or until the apples are tender, turning them occasionally during cooking and spooning the sauce over the tops. Serve warm, with the sauce spooned over the apples, or allow to cool and chill in the sauce until ready to serve. Garnish with mint, if desired.

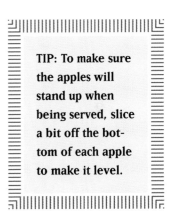

TIP: To make sure the apples will stand up when being served, slice a bit off the bottom of each apple to make it level.

Christmas "Lights"

When you ask people what comes to mind when they think about Christmas, usually food is high on the list. And what foods do people think of? Some imagine a big, juicy turkey with creamy mashed potatoes and savory gravy. Others envision trays piled high with Christmas cookies like holiday cutouts and gingerbread people and loads of yummy sweet treats.

Whatever our favorite foods are, one thing's for sure—if we aren't careful, our belts will get a little bit tighter from all the good cheer during the Yuletide season. You know, a little bite here and a little snack there all add up. So it's a good thing that we have lots of ways to watch ourselves around this time. One of the ways is to enjoy a Christmas dinner that's lighter than a traditional one. Here's my menu of quick-and-easy holiday dishes that I call Christmas "Lights." Go ahead and enjoy—with less guilt!

Scallion-Garlic Soup

4 to 6 servings

Looking for a way to start the Christmas meal with something light that has lots of flavor and is easy to prepare, too? Here's the answer to our Christmas wishes—a scallion-garlic soup that's loaded with flavor and is ready in just minutes.

8 garlic cloves, minced

3 cans (14½ ounces each) ready-to-use chicken broth

1½ cups water

4 slices stale or toasted bread, cut into ½-inch cubes

½ teaspoon black pepper

2 egg whites, beaten

3 scallions, thinly sliced

Coat a large saucepan with nonstick cooking spray. Add the garlic and lightly brown over medium heat, stirring constantly. Add the broth, water, bread, and pepper; mix well. Bring to a boil, then reduce the heat to low. Remove 2 tablespoons of the soup to a small bowl and combine with the egg whites. Using a fork, slowly stir the egg-white mixture into the soup, forming egg strands. Cook for 4 to 5 minutes, or until heated through. Ladle into individual bowls, top with the sliced scallions, and serve immediately.

GREAT GO-ALONG: Cut a garlic clove in half crosswise and rub over toasted slices of French bread.

Did You Know . . . the average person burns up over 500 calories per hour "running" through the mall? See, you knew shopping was good for you!

Pull-Apart Herbed Rolls

1 dozen rolls

Herbs and spices are a super way to add an extra kick to any dish without adding lots of inches to our waists, so these tasty rolls are perfect for dunking in scallion-garlic soup (or any other kind of soup).

¼ cup canola oil
¼ cup chopped fresh parsley
2 tablespoons grated Parmesan cheese
½ teaspoon dried thyme
½ teaspoon onion powder
2 loaves (1 pound each) frozen bread dough, thawed and cut into 1-inch cubes

Coat a 12-cup muffin tin with nonstick cooking spray. In a large bowl, combine all the ingredients except the dough; mix well. Add the dough and toss to coat completely. Place the dough in the muffin cups, cover, and allow to rise for 40 minutes, or until doubled in size. Preheat the oven to 375°F. Bake for 25 to 30 minutes, or until golden brown.

Champagne-Roasted Turkey

6 to 8 servings

Why wait until New Year's Eve to break out the champagne? We can make a real holiday treat by using it to baste our Christmas turkey. The results are the true test—moist, tasty, and very light . . . every time! When a lighter dish can taste this good, it's easy to start early on a New Year's resolution to eat lighter!

½ pound red seedless grapes, stemmed and cut in half (about 1½ cups), divided
One 7- to 7½-pound bone-in turkey breast
½ teaspoon salt
½ teaspoon black pepper
1 bottle (750 ml) champagne (see Tip)
1 can (14½ ounces) ready-to-use chicken broth
2 tablespoons cornstarch

Preheat the oven to 350°F. Line a roasting pan with aluminum foil and coat the aluminum foil with nonstick cooking spray. Place the turkey in the pan and spoon 1 cup grape halves into the neck cavity. Season the turkey all over with the salt and pepper. Pour the champagne into the pan around the turkey. Bake for 2¼ to 2½ hours, or until no pink remains and the juices run clear, basting every 30 minutes with the pan juices. If the turkey begins to get too brown, cover loosely with aluminum foil. In a medium saucepan, combine the chicken broth, cornstarch, and pan drippings with fat removed; bring to a boil over medium-high heat, stirring constantly until thickened. Stir in the remaining grape halves and cook for 1 to 2 minutes, or until heated through. Carve the turkey and serve with the champagne grape sauce.

TIP: You can use a nonalcoholic sparkling wine or cider in place of the champagne.

Holiday Charlotte

8 to 10 servings

Grace the holiday table with a side dish that's a little different and a little lighter, too. Best of all, it's easy to prepare!

1 pound orzo pasta
2 tablespoons butter, melted
1 can (4 ounces) sliced mushrooms or mushroom stems and pieces, drained
1 jar (2 ounces) diced pimientos, drained
2 scallions, thinly sliced
2 envelopes (a 2-ounce box) onion soup mix

TIP: Fill the center with a bunch of curly parsley to add some nice color to your table!

Preheat the oven to 350°F. Cook the orzo according to the package directions; drain. Place in a large bowl; stir in the melted butter. Add the mushrooms, pimientos, scallions, and onion soup mix; mix well. Place in a 10-inch Bundt or tube pan and bake for 25 to 30 minutes, or until heated through. Invert onto a serving platter. Serve immediately.

Cranberry-Stuffed Squash

4 servings

TIP: For a crunchy topping, sprinkle ½ cup finely chopped pecans over the cranberry sauce before baking.

When you first set this on the table, nobody will know whether you're serving cranberry sauce in an acorn squash bowl or baked acorn squash glazed with cranberry sauce. But they'll find out soon enough that it's a tasty, festive-looking squash and cranberry side dish. Mmm!

2 tablespoons butter, melted
2 medium acorn squash, cut in half and seeded
¼ teaspoon salt
1 can (16 ounces) whole-berry cranberry sauce

Did You Know . . . pulling out the Christmas decorations can be a healthy workout? Sure, it's good for us to stretch up to those hard-to-reach places and bend to the lower ones. Just be careful and don't overdo it!

Preheat the oven to 400°F. Line a rimmed baking sheet with aluminum foil. Brush the butter evenly over each squash half, then sprinkle with the salt. Place on the baking sheet and bake for 45 minutes. Spoon the cranberry sauce equally into the centers of the squash halves and bake for 25 to 30 more minutes, or until the squash is tender.

Sweet-and-Sour Cabbage

6 to 8 servings

Steamed cabbage is a winner every time, especially when it's got the extra flavor of this sweet-and-sour version. Plus, it's a nice change from the traditional green veggies that are served on holiday menus.

1 medium head red cabbage, shredded
2 medium apples, chopped
1 medium onion, chopped
½ cup cider vinegar
¼ cup firmly packed light brown sugar
¼ teaspoon ground cloves
½ teaspoon salt

In a soup pot, combine all the ingredients and bring to a boil over medium-high heat. Reduce the heat to low, cover, and simmer for 40 to 50 minutes, or until the cabbage is tender.

Lemon-Glazed Angel Food Cake

12 to 16 servings

How appropriate—an angel food cake for Christmas. Why, it's light, it's quick, and boy, is it heavenly. Drizzled with your own lemon glaze, this one's sure to become the most popular dessert on the table!

2 cups sugar, divided
1 cup all-purpose flour
12 egg whites
1½ teaspoons cream of tartar
1 teaspoon vanilla extract
¼ teaspoon salt
¼ cup fresh lemon juice
1 tablespoon grated lemon peel

TIP: Sprinkle the top of the cake with a dozen finely crushed lemon drops for an extra zesty taste.

Preheat the oven to 375°F. In a medium bowl, combine ¾ cup sugar and the flour; mix well and set aside. In a large bowl, beat the egg whites, cream of tartar, vanilla, and salt until soft peaks form. Slowly add ¾ cup sugar and beat until stiff peaks form. Fold the flour mixture gently into the egg-white mixture until thoroughly combined. Pour into an ungreased tube pan and bake for 35 to 40 minutes, or until the top is golden and dry. Invert the cake in the pan onto a wire rack and allow to cool completely. Remove from the pan and place on a serving plate. In a small

Did You Know . . .
it's simple to work off extra holiday calories during work? Try taking the stairs instead of the elevator, or get off a few floors early and walk the rest of the way. "Every little bit helps!"

saucepan, bring the lemon juice, lemon peel, and the remaining ½ cup sugar to a boil over medium heat. Boil for 2 to 3 minutes, or until the sugar has dissolved and the glaze is smooth, stirring occasionally. Remove from the heat and drizzle over the cake just before serving.

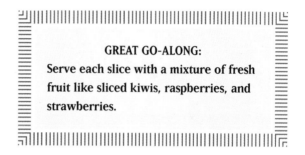

GREAT GO-ALONG:
Serve each slice with a mixture of fresh fruit like sliced kiwis, raspberries, and strawberries.

Quick Meals

For many of us, the weeks and days leading up to Christmas are the most stressful time of the year. I mean, between buying and wrapping presents, sending cards, baking cookies, cleaning and decorating the house, and all the other holiday preparations, who has any extra time or energy for putting a hot and healthy meal on the table every night?!

I know it seems easier to have pizza delivered or to pick up burgers and fries at the drive-thru on the way home from work, but "homemade" doesn't always mean lots of work. With just a couple of ingredients and a few minutes of our time, we can make some tasty meals . . . completely hassle-free! And, even better, they give us a way to get the rest of the family to help out, too. Let them set the table and make a tossed salad. Then you can sit together as a family and enjoy your quick meal with some of the togetherness that's so often sacrificed on the days leading up to Christmas. It may even be the perfect chance to drop some last-minute hints for Santa's shopping list!

Quick Lasagna Toss

6 to 8 servings

There's nothing more mouthwatering than homemade lasagna oozing with cheese. It's not impossible to enjoy those yummy long-cooked flavors during this hectic time. We can, thanks to a few shortcuts.

12 lasagna noodles, broken into large pieces
1 pound hot Italian sausage, casings removed
1 jar (26 ounces) spaghetti sauce
1 cup ricotta cheese
2 cups (8 ounces) shredded mozzarella cheese
½ cup grated Parmesan cheese
½ teaspoon dried basil
½ teaspoon black pepper

TIP: A sprinkle of chopped parsley before serving, and this will look extra-fancy and fresh.

Cook the noodles according to the package directions; drain. Meanwhile, in a soup pot, cook the sausage over medium-high heat for 6 to 8 minutes, or until no pink remains, stirring to crumble the sausage; drain the fat from the pot. Add the noodles and the remaining ingredients; mix well. Reduce the heat to medium-low and cook for 6 to 8 minutes, or until heated through and the cheese has melted. Serve immediately.

Did You Know . . .
you deserve a present, too? Absolutely! After all that cleaning, cooking, decorating, and shopping, why not spoil yourself by spending an afternoon doing whatever makes you happiest?

Skillet Shepherd's Pie

4 to 6 servings

We're not going to wait an hour for dinner tonight. In just minutes it'll be ready and waiting!

- 2 cups cubed cooked chicken
- 1 package (16 ounces) frozen mixed vegetables, thawed and drained
- 1 can (10¾ ounces) condensed cream of chicken soup
- ½ cup milk
- ¼ teaspoon onion powder
- ¼ teaspoon black pepper
- 4 cups hot mashed potatoes (instant or leftover)

TIP: Use leftover chicken or turn to the deli case for thick-cut turkey breast.

In a large skillet, combine all the ingredients except the potatoes over high heat; mix well. Cook for 5 to 8 minutes, or until heated through, stirring frequently. Remove from the heat and dollop with the potatoes. Serve immediately.

Seafood Minestrone

10 to 14 servings

Soups are probably the easiest and heartiest dishes we could prepare for quick-and-easy dinners. You see, we can make this minestrone on Sunday and leave it in the fridge for a few nights. Then, during the week, we can reheat it a bowl or two at a time as we need it. With hot, crusty rolls and some bagged salad . . . voilà! We can have dinner in just twenty minutes. That leaves us more time to shop!

3 cans (14½ ounces each) ready-to-use beef broth
1 can (28 ounces) crushed tomatoes
1 can (19 ounces) garbanzo beans (chick peas), undrained
1 can (15¼ ounces) red kidney beans, undrained
1 package (16 ounces) frozen mixed vegetables, thawed
1 package (10 ounces) frozen chopped spinach, thawed and drained
1 small onion, chopped
1 teaspoon garlic powder
1 teaspoon salt
½ teaspoon black pepper
1 cup uncooked elbow macaroni
1 pound fresh or frozen white-fleshed fish fillets, such as cod, haddock, or whiting, cut into 1-inch chunks
1 pound fresh shrimp, peeled and deveined

Did You Know . . . you can make things easier for yourself by eliminating last-minute kitchen chores? Several weeks before the holidays, chop a bunch of onions and freeze them in a plastic bag. Do the same with other frequently used holiday ingredients, such as celery, green peppers, and garlic. It'll really help when you're pinched for time later.

170

In a large soup pot, combine the broth, crushed tomatoes, garbanzo beans, kidney beans, mixed vegetables, spinach, onion, garlic powder, salt, and pepper. Bring to a boil over high heat, then stir in the macaroni. Reduce the heat to low and simmer for 15 minutes, or until the macaroni is tender. Add the fish and shrimp and simmer for 5 to 7 minutes, or until the fish flakes easily with a fork and the shrimp turn pink, stirring occasionally.

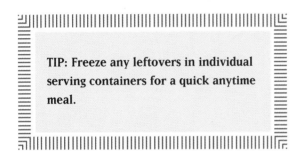

TIP: Freeze any leftovers in individual serving containers for a quick anytime meal.

State Fair Pasta

6 to 8 servings

It's been months since most of us have tasted one of those hot sausage and pepper sandwiches that we get at fairs. I always love the taste of those sandwiches, but it's December and the next fair isn't for some time. Too bad, right? *Wrong!* I combined those flavors into a quick meal by substituting pasta for the bread and adding spaghetti sauce. And it's easy to give it a festive touch—use pasta shaped like bells, stars, or even Christmas trees.

1 pound rigatoni, penne, or shaped Christmas pasta (see Tip)
2 pounds hot Italian turkey sausage, casings removed
3 large bell peppers (1 each red, green, and yellow), cut into 1-inch chunks
1 large onion, chopped
1 can (28 ounces) diced tomatoes
1 jar (26 ounces) spaghetti sauce
2 tablespoons tomato paste
½ teaspoon black pepper

TIP: Pasta shaped like Christmas trees is available in the supermarket pasta section and Christmas shops during the holiday season.

Prepare the pasta according to the package directions; drain. Meanwhile, in a soup pot, sauté the sausage, bell peppers, and onion over medium-high heat for 6 to 8 minutes, or until the vegetables are tender and no pink remains in the sausage. Add the remaining ingredients and cook for 5 minutes, or until heated through and bubbly. Spoon over the pasta and serve.

Peachy Pork Chops

4 servings

This recipe was created totally by accident. A viewer told me he had just finished cooking pork chops and was carrying the pan over to the kitchen counter. Well, his wife had just opened a can of peaches for a fruit salad she was making and . . . crash! You guessed it—they had pork chops smothered in peaches. Instead of tossing the meal into the garbage, they shrugged their shoulders and dug in. Yum, what a taste! I'm sure you'll agree that this dish is no accident.

4 pork loin chops (1½ to 2 pounds total), about 1 inch thick
½ teaspoon salt
¼ teaspoon black pepper
1 tablespoon vegetable oil
1 can (15¼ ounces) sliced peaches in heavy syrup
2 tablespoons light brown sugar
1 teaspoon ground ginger
4 cups hot cooked rice

Season both sides of the pork chops with the salt and pepper. Heat the oil in a large skillet over medium-high heat and brown the pork chops for 3 to 4 minutes per side. Stir in the remaining ingredients except the rice. Reduce the heat to medium and simmer for 15 to 20 minutes, or until the pork chops are cooked through and the sauce has thickened. Serve over the rice.

The Big Sandwich

6 servings

Here's a winning recipe from the National Beef Cook-Off that's just perfect for this time of year. One of the contest rules is that the recipes must be quick and easy, and this one is! It's a yummy combo of roast beef, red peppers, pesto sauce, feta cheese, and mixed greens, served up on a loaf of fresh bread. The best part is that it's served cold, so it can be ready in no time no matter *what* time we start dinner.

> TIP: Depending on your super-market or bakery, round breads should be readily available. If they aren't, just call and ask them to make one for you.

1 round loaf (12 inches) French or Italian bread

⅓ cup mayonnaise

3 tablespoons prepared pesto sauce

1 teaspoon fresh lemon juice

1 pound thinly sliced deli roast beef

1 jar (7 ounces) roasted red peppers, well drained

½ cup (3 ounces) crumbled feta cheese

1 package (4 ounces) mixed baby greens

Cut the bread horizontally in half and remove the center from both halves, leaving a 1-inch-thick shell. In a small bowl, combine the mayonnaise, pesto sauce, and lemon juice; mix well. Spread over the cut surface of each bread half. Layer the roast beef, roasted peppers, cheese, and greens over the bottom half of the bread. Replace the top and cut into six wedges. Serve immediately, or wrap in plastic wrap and chill for up to 2 hours before serving.

> **Did You Know . . .**
> if each of us reused wrapping paper or used newspaper as a wrap on just *three* gifts, the paper we save would cover forty-five thousand football fields?! That's because the average American consumer wraps twenty gifts each year at the holidays. Why not make recycling a holiday priority and, by doing that, give ourselves a gift that really makes a difference?

175

Lo Mein Soup

6 to 8 servings

TIP: Top each bowl with some crispy noodles.

Chinese take-out is always popular during the holidays, 'cause it's as easy as a phone call. Well, what if I told you I had a recipe that takes less time than ordering and picking up? By the time everyone agrees on what they want, you'll be serving up steaming bowls of lo mein soup. Heat up some frozen egg rolls and have a few fortune cookies for dessert for a "Column-A Special" that you can call your very own.

> 4 cans (14½ ounces each) ready-to-use chicken broth
> 2 cups water
> 1 package (16 ounces) frozen stir-fry vegetable mix, thawed
> ½ pound boneless, skinless chicken breast, cut into ½-inch chunks
> ¼ pound fresh mushrooms, thinly sliced
> 2 tablespoons light soy sauce
> ½ pound spaghetti, broken in half

In a soup pot, combine all the ingredients except the spaghetti; bring to a boil over medium-high heat. Add the spaghetti and boil for 8 to 10 minutes, or until the spaghetti is cooked and no pink remains in the chicken.

BLT Burritos

4 burritos

No need to do the Mexican fast food drive-thru routine when you can have a fiesta right at home without any fuss. Just fold up some quick-and-easy burritos and practice that international Christmas carol, "Feliz Navidad," as you enjoy this fast homemade dinner.

6 cups shredded iceberg lettuce
1 medium ripe tomato, chopped
1 cup mayonnaise
1 container (3 ounces) real bacon bits (see Tip)
⅛ teaspoon black pepper
Four 10-inch flour tortillas

In a large bowl, combine the lettuce, tomato, mayonnaise, bacon bits, and pepper; mix well. Spoon the mixture evenly into the centers of the tortillas. Fold up the bottom of each tortilla over the lettuce mixture, then fold both sides over envelope fashion. Fold the top of each tortilla over and turn seam side down. Serve immediately.

TIP: No bacon bits on hand? Chop ¼ pound of deli turkey and mix it in, creating a "TLT" burrito.

Did You Know . . . one of the most popular spots for tourists in New York City during the month of December is Rockefeller Center, where the famed Christmas tree stands? The tree is usually over ninety feet tall and holds tens of thousands of lights. The Rockefeller Center tree is a tradition that began in 1933.

Make-Ahead Hungarian Beef Stew

4 to 6 servings

If you don't have a slow cooker, you'd better make sure to add one to your Christmas list so you won't miss out on meals like this one. It's so helpful to be able to cut up everything the night before and store it in the refrigerator. Then you just place it in the slow cooker in the morning and let it cook! Eight hours later, when everybody's starved for dinner, you've got a long-cooked savory stew that's ready for the table!

3 medium potatoes, peeled and cut into 1-inch chunks
2 large onions, cut into large chunks
5 medium carrots, cut into 1-inch chunks
1 package (10 ounces) frozen lima beans, thawed
2 pounds beef stew meat or boneless chuck roast, cut into 1½-inch chunks
1 can (14½ ounces) diced tomatoes
½ cup beef broth
2 garlic cloves, minced
2 tablespoons paprika
1½ teaspoons salt
½ cup instant mashed potato flakes
1 cup sour cream

In a 3½-quart (or larger) slow cooker, combine the potatoes, onions, carrots, and lima beans; mix well. In a large bowl, combine the meat, tomatoes, broth, garlic, paprika, and salt; place over the vegetables in the slow cooker. Cover and cook on the low setting for 8 to 10 hours, until the meat is fork-tender. Stir in the potato flakes until well mixed and the stew has thickened. Just before serving, stir in the sour cream.

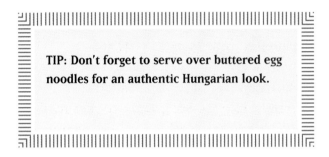

TIP: Don't forget to serve over buttered egg noodles for an authentic Hungarian look.

Corn Soup

4 to 6 servings

Imagine a soup that has just four ingredients and is ready in under ten minutes! Here it is, creamy and satisfying. What a perfect meal for those nights when you've been shopping at the mall and want something light, yet a little hearty, with very little effort.

2 cans (14¾ ounces each) cream-style corn
1⅔ cups milk
2 tablespoons butter
¼ teaspoon black pepper

In a large saucepan, combine all the ingredients over medium heat. Cook for 5 to 7 minutes, or until heated through, stirring frequently.

CHRISTMAS CARD LIST

Name	Address

CHRISTMAS CARD LIST

Name	Address

GIFT LOG

Name	Gift	Thank You

GIFT LOG

Name	Gift	Thank You

Index

Mr. Food®'s Library Gives You More Ways to Say...

"OOH IT'S SO GOOD!!"®

W I L L I A M   M O R R O W

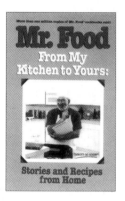

Q

R

S

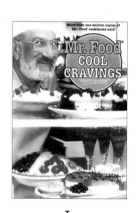

T

U

V

W

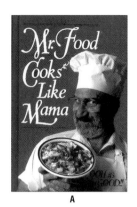

A

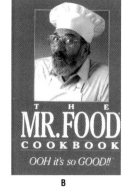

B

C

D

E

F

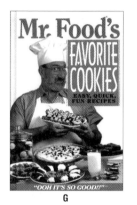

G

H

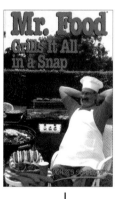

I

J

K

L

M

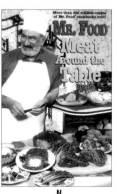

N

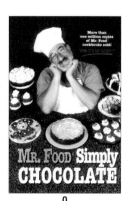

O

P

LOOKING FOR THE PERFECT HOLIDAY GIFTS?

HERE THEY ARE!

TITLE	PRICE	QUANTITY
A. **Mr. Food** Cooks Like Mama	@ $14.95 each	x _____ = $_____
B. The **Mr. Food** Cookbook, *OOH IT'S SO GOOD!!*	@ $14.95 each	x _____ = $_____
C. **Mr. Food** Cooks Chicken	@ $ 9.95 each	x _____ = $_____
D. **Mr. Food** Cooks Pasta	@ $ 9.95 each	x _____ = $_____
E. **Mr. Food** Makes Dessert	@ $ 9.95 each	x _____ = $_____
F. **Mr. Food** Cooks Real American	@ $14.95 each	x _____ = $_____
G. **Mr. Food** 's Favorite Cookies	@ $11.95 each	x _____ = $_____
H. **Mr. Food** 's Quick and Easy Side Dishes	@ $11.95 each	x _____ = $_____
I. **Mr. Food** Grills It All in a Snap	@ $11.95 each	x _____ = $_____
J. **Mr. Food** 's Fun Kitchen Tips and Shortcuts (and Recipes, Too!)	@ $11.95 each	x _____ = $_____
K. **Mr. Food** 's Old World Cooking Made Easy	@ $14.95 each	x _____ = $_____
L. "Help, **Mr. Food** ! Company's Coming!"	@ $14.95 each	x _____ = $_____
M. **Mr. Food** Pizza 1-2-3	@ $12.00 each	x _____ = $_____
N. **Mr. Food** Meat Around the Table	@ $12.00 each	x _____ = $_____
O. **Mr. Food** Simply Chocolate	@ $12.00 each	x _____ = $_____
P. **Mr. Food** A Little Lighter	@ $14.95 each	x _____ = $_____
Q. **Mr. Food** From My Kitchen to Yours: Stories and Recipes from Home	@ $14.95 each	x _____ = $_____
R. **Mr. Food** Easy Tex-Mex	@ $11.95 each	x _____ = $_____
S. **Mr. Food** One Pot, One Meal	@ $11.95 each	x _____ = $_____
T. **Mr. Food** Cool Cravings: Easy Chilled and Frozen Desserts	@ $11.95 each	x _____ = $_____
U. **Mr. Food** 's Italian Kitchen	@ $14.95 each	x _____ = $_____
V. **Mr. Food** 's Simple Southern Favorites	@ $14.95 each	x _____ = $_____
W. A **Mr. Food** Christmas: Homemade and Hassle-Free	@ $19.95 each	x _____ = $_____

Send payment to:
Mr. Food
P.O. Box 9227
Coral Springs, FL 33075-9227

Name _____

Street _____ Apt._____

City _____ State_____ Zip_____

Method of Payment: ☐ Check or ☐ Money Order Enclosed

Please allow up to 6 weeks for delivery.

Book Total	$_____
+ Postage & Handling for *First Copy*	$ 4.00
+ $1 Postage & Handling for Ea. Add'l. Copy (Canadian Orders Add Add'l. $2.00 *Per Copy*)	$_____
Subtotal	$_____
Add 6% Sales Tax (FL Residents Only)	$_____
Total in U.S. Funds	$_____

BKW1